AF581599

~~Un~~holy Blood

Writer : Radha Paudel

Translator : Umesh Bajagain

Publisher : Radha Paudel Foundation

Cover : Suman Maharjan

ISBN : 978-9937-1-3194-0

To her,

Who bled from deep to death,

Left to die in barns and bed-cold

Disregarded, Domineered, Oppressed

Your legacy shall live forever

Even though you did not

Preface to the English Translation

We could not materialize the planned schedule for bringing the English version of Apabitra Ragat on its second anniversary because of the unstoppable COVID. Circumstances altered the course of events but did so only for the better.

This book has attacked, and rightly so, the entrenched malpractices and ignorance that surround menstruation. When it first came out, it shook the mutual non-disclosure agreement amongst people about menstruation-to the dismay of many in schools, universities, literary circles, social activists, and the like, both home and abroad. Some were engaged in the definitional conundrum of what counts as literature, while others were enraged, keen to "see you in the court." They regurgitated on their own reluctant words, barely expressed views on newspapers, let alone the courtesy of congratulations.

That was the far side of the moon, the dark side of the moon as they say. The bright side is what kept me going. Some people wrote to me with open hearts letters of love and agony and commendation and longed for mentorship with pride. Some titled me 'the Taslima Nasrin' of Nepal. I had promised that I'd accept everything under the sun, and I did. I'm grateful for both souls.

Heaps of feminine agonies still lay on the slush pile of challenges, in mutated forms. Yet, it wouldn't be justifiable if we say nothing good has happened in the journey towards Dignified Menstruation (DM); it has. Even so, hardly weeks go by when I do not feel for those who lost their lives in the sheds, both squalid and affluent, in the pursuit of a dignified living, rights they were denied since civilization.

I am thankful to all those who've lent their hands both at home and abroad and gifted love, appreciation, suggestions, mercy, respect, and solidarity. It has only been possible to move forward in this bog with those hands on our hands.

Menstruators in their pursuit of dignity have reached a milestone in 2019 when Radha Paudel Foundation not just led to frame the Global South Coalition for Dignified Menstruation, but also started observing December 8 as Dignified Menstruation Day. On the occasion of the second Dignified Menstruation Day, the foundation released a book Dignified Menstruation: A Practical Hand-Book-a white paper on Dignified Menstruation-along with the declaration of 12-point manifesto borne out of 3-day International Dignified Menstruation Workshop held on December 8-10, 2020. This program was jointly organized by the Ministry of Women, Children, and Senior Citizens and the Nepal Human Rights Commission, and in which the Ministry of Health, Education, and Water Supply and Women Commission along with 70 other organizations and networks from all over the world partook of the event.

Aligned with Dignified Menstruation, Dignified Menopause, a Global Perspective planned for 8th December 2021 in collaboration with partners from and in UK.

Dignified Menstruation is a new concept overlooked by human rights, women's rights, and development movements for decades. It is that gigantic elephant in the room everyone chose to neglect. DM reinvokes the vitality of menstruation as the ultimate life-kindling force in the universe-earth, so far, we know-and factors in cultural, social, economic, political, environmental, and other multidimensional aspects while making sense of menstruation. DM ascertains the rights of a menstruator to earn a dignified living and that of a non-menstruator to be self-aware of those rights.

However, it is easier said than done. To change a world, and more, its people entrenched with dogma, orthodox, reluctance, and ignorance for decades, is indeed no piece of cake. What's more difficult is if the call for change originates from a village-born woman of a 'third-world' country-understandably, this appeal disrupts certain political and emotional channels. But now it has started, it is inexorable. There are more hands laid out in solidarity day in, day out. The campaign is far from deferred, only inevitable every day.

It's not because we think it is easy that we have continued in the journey but that it's difficult but worth it. I salute those hands who've been together in this fight all along and who've lent theirs. I appeal to all human beings of this beautiful world-readers and stakeholders alike, through this book-to partake of the investigation, capacity building, lobbying, and materialization of the rights of every menstrurators on this earth.

In the end, I would be forever indebted to Umesh Bajagain for translating this book and Kathmandu Publication for holding accountability by taking responsibility of publication.

On Apabitra Ragat

I want to thank you from my heart's bottom for choosing this book. Why you bought this book may be different-you like it; a friend suggested; you're curious, or you're an avid reader. Here's my disclaimer: depending on who you are, you might get offended by many of the things presented here. If you're offended or provoked, please defer your emotions until the end. And after reading it, call or email me and tell me how you feel. You may want to rant about it on social media or even lodge a case in court. I expect these emotions and am more than willing to listen to you.

Or maybe you won't be affected by it, or will be deeply moved; whatever it is you feel, at the end of the book, I urge you to use your unbiased compass and make a table with two columns and write your name on one and mine on the other. Then, write both our arguments. I'm sure you'd be convinced with mine in a majority of the cases if not all.

In case you read the entire book, I also urge you to close your eyes and imagine yourself in the `isolation' those thousands of women live(d) in, and die(d) due to menstruation. I urge you to feel the huffs and puffs of God-knows-what during the night when you're dreaming in your cozy bed. And ask yourself-what your mothers, sisters, daughters, and wives have put up with and condition they're in. Ask yourself what as a country we have become, or are supposed to be? How did we go wrong? How much have we lost? Should it have been like Tista and Kaangada? The answer is there. You just have to seek them.

If you want to explore more, the handbook Dignified Menstruation: Everyone's Business will help you get a vantage-glimpse of the issue. That way, you'll be able to come close to what I see from here.

I did not write this book for the riches it'll bring. Or because I want to be popular. It is but my attempt to consolidate all my agony, rage, courage, pride, celebration, power, and inferiority complex I garnered since the day I was blood-subordinated. Smeared. I have lived the good days; I have lived the bad days. I have encountered those who've seen them, listened, and breathed with them. I might have named some people and organizations in the course of writing this book. But I intend to write nothing but the truth.

And if it hurts, well, I should say I'm sorry.

Like Jumla: A Nurse's Story was a fraction of my life, this book is a quarter that attempts to draw on my works on Dignified Menstruation. A quarter is not whole-there's still much to write-and a whole in its entirety cannot be written. With its multidimensional facets, from a single vantage point, it is difficult to write everything and anything. As far as I'm concerned, I'm just a speck in the menstruating universe.

As much as my life has been a story, I'm sure so has yours. I'm confident, in your story, there's at least a mother, wife, daughter, sister, neighbor, or you who's had to live an undignified life-in a squalid shed of the rustic or a cozy bed of the glitterati-just away from the loved ones. No matter what it is, they always end up shaggy or lost in confidence and with blown self-esteem.

Give them this book as a gift. I've attempted to write for them, and tell them they're not alone, not weak at all-empowered by all means. Because they're the ones who bore the humans.

I thank everyone who carried this book on their backs, especially those who've lived inside this book, true to its every ounce.

Before adieu, I wish you all the best for your next #dignified-menstruation-talk in your family. And after that, congratulations-you broke a chain that will break more chains in the future.

Radha Paudel
Gauriganj, Bharatpur-8, Chitwan
Aug 4, 2018
Email: rpaudel456@gmail.com
rpaudelfoundation@gmail.com
www.radhapaudelfoundation.org

The Pursuit of Dignity

When I flopped on the floor, a small pouch I'd been carrying sat with me. My body tried several postures in an anxious attempt of recuperation but no matter how I crossed my legs, a lump of suffocation deep inside had stuck, waiting to make me cry all my remaining tears out. I won't say I didn't weep. But I didn't wail. My chest fluttered palpitating the major blood vessels in my body. A tsunami of waves translated into colorless crystal volcanos in my eyes and tried their hands on me but failed. The vehicles voyaged my eyesight in the Mahendra highway, heedless to my suffering.

A mist blurred my vision like the water-dispensing fog hiding away its treasured blue sky. The anxiety-driven tears that aspired relentlessly unable to force themselves through my eyes finally squashed down my throat. I ended up getting more anatomical to smother the anxiety: I didn't let a bit of waste supposed to exit my body inside my body. That way I suppose I won.

But did I? Was this triviality my real victory? Of course not. Unless I had succeeded defending my own blood, which I couldn't. I was incensed at the loss I bore at my own behest. And I pity my mind for not being able to swallow what I should have, for good. I can't help but feel sorry for myself.

I am a naïve woman by all means. Naïve enough to shout over the darkness when it's the light that leaves me.

That naïve. I should have snuggled what I went thorugh into the deepest parts of my heart. But like a crazy unstoppable woman, I couldn't hide stuff inside me.

The clouds that flew in my zenith have gone darker in a way segregated from the rest, like a dark patch on a white loincloth, like smudged and blackened. The sun was not mine today. It teased me and the colour I was in. I stretched my head back in my body and gazed at the dark blue tissue strata I had formed, gathered the frock I wore with my hands, and inspected between my legs. I could see it there.

My body stood on a pavement of a serpentine road with two lanes across which were bushes followed by thickets of green, as lost as a touch-me-not waning its every single leaf. I was the touch-me-not. Each drop from my eyes forced the mimosa's leaves to fall back like soldiers in a do-or-die battle. I cut off the torment those innocent leaves had to bear on their part, wiped my tears wide until ears, and registered their wet mark on my hands and onto the clumsy grass. They were my own-dry stumps of rural grass and the tender strubs yet lovelier than the Majesty's estate, the altitude of which I could relate. My amorphous mind transcended from annoyance to loveliness, and fidgety suffocation to love. The shrubs cajoled me to remain true with my feelings.

"Relax. There's no need to be ashamed," they said.

Towards the north is the District Administration office. In the south, you'll see the residential kingpin corner, the Hakimchowk. And in the interstice between these two live the patrons-of-intoxication ready to abandon their huts as the nights plummet. The place speaks of the blood-smeared angels-those wounded by the ferocious notoreity of these

kingpins and patrons-and pretends to be a shelter for the cupid bastards germinated and forced out of them. It's a common breeding ground to all-everyone and everything. Tears, urine, faeces, blood, vomit, and every bit of shit: a tree rest-stop to everything.

There are two kinds of people around me: the one at the top-the monkeys, and the other on the ground-the ants. The taller people at the top-the monkeys-have a hard time seeing what's wriggling on the ground. They can't see the ants. But the ants enjoy the monkey's musicals. The tall-sitters can't view the ones sitting below because their eyes are fixed at the torso or the hunger-belly of the world. The crawlers and the wrigglers and the walkers reign in their blind spot disregarded. I don't have those eyes at least. I don't have the spot. The blind spot. Because I belong from below. And I see things.

And in my world below, I have all kinds of beings. The most enduring is the Dubo, the Bermuda grass. I have seen my mother dry her secret clothes on this grass. People pluck this Dubo from its world of underground and elevate it sacramentally onto God's feet. Lucky plant to have elevated at all. Just like that. I have meticulously counted seven sacred Dubo shoots myself and offered it to the Almighty. From garlands around people's neck onto their chests to people's anal pores wiping their feces, the dubo plant sometimes falls and at other times elevates.

Sorry but I haven't introduced myself. I am that Burmuda grass, long story cut short. I am Dubo. Few days a year, I'm a goddess-I belong to the elevated. And during the rest, I'm the wriggling creature below the monkeys don't see.

When I had no idea about personal hygiene, I too was the one to wipe-scrub my butt and blood onto these turfs in a typical animalistic pose. My hands joined the feet, and I scent-rubbed myself with an ephemeral sense of hygiene. A sense of self-driven primitive coziness.

Driven-I've started only with the thought that I remembered I was driven too. I ran away from home-it's an hour ago truth-not everyone knows and not the strangest things of all I've done, but I can't lie to myself I'm driven away by my own parents, sisters, and villagers.

Father!

I tried to receive all the light that the farthest of the Mahendra highway could bestow on my eyes. Still nothing. Toward the west, I scanned for a man, a male, thin and tall with a Dhaka cap, on a bicycle thoroughfaring my way to be my father. But there was no sign of a man. I had this strong urge to see my father whom I was forbidden to see-just to get the heck of it-to try and see what devastation awaits ahead. I demand to see who came up with such a stupid practice. Was it a man or a woman, I wonder!

Sure it must be a man, a being who enjoys his vanity of valor just as much exhibited when he moans on a prick of a thorn. Say hello to men who cry upon the rupture of the tiniest blood vessel in the body.

Oh my god, my nose bled. Take me to the hospital.

Put a woman to that equivalent. The degree that women bleed is out of comparison to be able to empathize that. I'm sure men don't acknowledge this because they envy this pain women can endure. They prohibit menstruating women to see their faces and maintain that women cannot and shouldn't exhibit a slightest sign of discomfort during the days when they bleed from their deep. I'm sure men must have forbidden women seeing them in their menstrual days for the fear of their sudden death, chronic discomfort, or the scourge that their lifespan could go short.

And guess what, women bought this gibberish in the name of tradition. But who doesn't panic on being told that they'll eat away their husband's living days-who stays most of the time out of sight-if they show up in the menstrual days before them? After all, life outside home is pretty arduous, to be honest. What if they actually die?

That's fine. But I can't be here!

If my father finds me strolling here, I'd be pancakes, battered as bad. It could be leftcheek-rightcheek greeting as well. Or maybe several to-and-fro swings of my long hair that usually gave in to my father. I can only guess from the available benevolent options. It depends whether you treat 'tied to a yoke all night sitting on a rock' as more or less generous as those slaps on your cheek.

That didn't, however, stop me giggling. I laughed at my own company which made trouble-making adventurous.

"Why did you run away like that? After all it's the same you've had to do like everyone does?" That might be my father.

Whatever happens, no matter how fumed Radha is, she will not cry today, I said to myself.

But isn't this all fascinating? That in absence of my father I can mock him all I want, all the time and not be punished? It was an utterly dissimilar story at home though.

Knock. Knock. "Open the door."

Hearing my father, my throat dried its last drop of spit as scorched by summer. At the moment, there were several neighboring brothers and sisters squatted on the floor; heads were up, voices talking and trading life scoops. The books were as read as torn on the floor. This was our home study group where we did everything but study.

My mother dozed on and off like a flickering light as if drugged in torpor in the west corner of the room. As soon as it seemed father had come at the door, my sister, who was beside the staircase, went for it like a meteor.

"Where's Radha," father summoned me as he climbed up the stairs.

"She has just been asleep, father. She was studying all this time." My sister replied in a faint voice.

I was but gossiping with my legs crossed in father's bed with family. Thank god my sister reported as I wished. I think I survived father's rage with a speck of remorse, not to mention the smile I was wearing.

That did not last longer.

"Asleep? Isn't it so early to go to bed you think? I have come in the midst of my veneration but what does she care?"

I was so frightened by father's words that I slipped beside my mother's back.

"Radha! Radha!" He shouted.

The house trembled at its corners. My bones felt a much higher jolt on the Richter scale from the inside. Mother must have felt it in my body; she started coughing. The spells were so violent we were afraid she'd somehow vomit her lungs out. It was a mysterious deep-down bark like a whooping cough. Anyone touches her or calls her name, the cough is gone.

"Such a silly child! Wake her up," father scowls in no particular direction.

"Radha! Wake up. Father's here." Sister kept knocking my body.

I was pretending hard to seem asleep. My breath was paused. My body acted like a dead leaf on a river. I had switched off my senses but I was not dead.

I doubted whether father is joining them to check whether I was asleep.

"Maybe she's asleep," mother said to sister. "Let it be."

Sister gave up and returned. I resumed my breathing in and out. It was a bit faster.

Ring, ring.

Some bell jingles startled me again. It could be father's bicycle but it was not; it was the rickshaw sailing along afar.

Oh god! I got to leave for my sister's. I'm getting late.

I have never been alone in this place, only with father and brother-in-law in a bicycle. Once, with mother on foot. The houses are farther apart here. Sparsely recurring patches of marsh and thickets fill in in between the houses. Mother warned me these places are not for girls. Hooligans hid in here for god knows what. I tried not to see around.

As the rickshaw puller passed by, he stared until our line of sight. It's easy for girls to fall into a black hole, different in shapes and sizes but the ultimate fate, always dark. This is the road to my sister. I'm sure there are no black hole tragectories in here, but who knows?

Does the rickshaw puller know me? I bet he does. He might steal me away with him. I've heard about these men who pierce into children's hearts, take them out, and eat them raw! If something like that is to happen, when exactly will I die?

It must be my mind engine. The rickshaw puller is my father's friend no doubt. What if he complains to father about my meandering?

I mapped a mental image of the way to my sister's home: Hakim Chowk, District Administration Office, Eye hospital, Bishal chowk, Kumaon Village, marshes, and then finally, sister's home. As easy as ABC.

I should get going. Stuck to my mental navigation, I followed its instructions step by step.

First, you need to stand up and lift your leg. Go straight ahead. Turn left. Turn right. Wait. Now turn left? Or right? Left it is.

The pouch I carried followed me wherever I went. When I'm ahead, the pouch is behind. And sometimes I followed it ahead.

I chose not to be entangled with anything between home and Hakim chowk. The road was familiar but I met nobody I knew. This is the same road which took us to the hospital. The road I chose to return after celebrating the life anniversaries of our late king and queen. The on-foot-road that avoided the jungle, and school if I'm unwilling. The very road which was the thoroughfare of hundreds of women marching to the river during the Rishi Panchami puja. This road never fails to fascinate me, even today.

Harlem at the River

Rishi Panchami always falls a day after Teej (pronounced as tiz) or two. I loved Teej festival for two reasons. One-that women could stay at home and escape work or school for a day. Two-women could binge-eat anything they want and men had to bring them over. Sweets, dishes, you name it! Teej is also known for its typical women-centered songs that flood the media. I composed few songs myself. There was a gobble-up-all-like-a-parrot attitude for the songs that Radio Nepal played. I learned them instantly and sang along until the sun no longer brightened our front yard.

It's a day's festival-Teej, calls on only after a year

I've got to visit my sister, fetch her home

I'll feed you well twice dear-it's a promise, even if that means borrowing.

Brothers sing the song.

We weren't allowed to sing Teej songs after Rishi Panchami. So we'd finish off brushing all our talents on the very day waiting for an entire year to visit back.

Every year, Rishi Panchami brought an entire day of exceptional splendor as women's cultural kitty parties bloomed aside the river. Women from all nooks gathered at the tree rest-stop after taking a bath at the village tap or well. The puja itself took place in under a resting tree or home frontyard, which I had no luck to see, lasted till late afternoon, and sometimes until sunset. Pujas in Narayani river bank or in urban places but had to finish off early; women had to return home far away and didn't have as much time as women in the village.

Mothers and sisters, the participants in the puja, returned home worn-out from the entire day veneration. Because I had not menstruated, I was to carry out the house chores that day. Mother always kept the ritual short in the Narayani river bank because she had asthma and could not fast the entire day. I sat back at home, and I mused their going into the waters of Narayani. Women use mysterious forces stopping the unstoppable flow of the mighty river, and at the end of the day, pluck the sun from the sky, split it into bits, and take them home only to release those clandestine pieces to the sky early in the morning before men woke. This was what I imagined.

Mother, however, returned early from the puja and with a face that disapproved of my imagination. So, to make sure something of that sort happened, I was allowed to join her one year on the day of Rishi Panchami. Mother was lucky, I assumed, having me as company; at least this should be true if not anything else.

When I reached the river bank, I saw hundreds of women splashing river water onto each other's face, cracking inappropriate jokes. I was an obvious pricking bone in the qabab. Nothing you imagine is ever true.

Mothers, and menstruating sisters, prepared for Rishi Panchami a couple of days early. They collected the twigs and branches of a typical plant called Datiun (chaff-flower; Achyranthes aspera), split them into sizeable fragments, few inches long, and packed them up in a bundle of 20–21 pieces with the strands of cogongrasses.

On the day of Rishi Panchami, they gathered essential items such as bundles of Datiun, changed clothes, and prepared items for the rite early in the morning. Then, they shot themselves toward the river for the annual religious 'exodus', where hundreds of women met and forgot their homes for a while. Mesmerized by the meandering Narayani river in the month of Bhadra, the women joined and lodged in the opposite banks as if to conquer the river all at once-though from far they looked like ants frightened to cross the river, waiting for a drop of leaf. Their reddish blood-filled bodies looked like blobs of masses stirring around in a necklace. Mother joined the near side of the river and expanded the necklace infinitesimally.

I was the human wardrobe for mother and her friends. I gathered their clothes, especially of mother's, and sat them with me all along until they finished off their rites. I sometimes made them my mat, sat on them as long as I could, and often treated them as pillows and rested my body. But I never stopped circumnavigating them for the fear of theft. The grand extravaganza at the Narayani River that evening enraptured me. Each year on this day my heart filled with joy and extravagance-the extravagance of the Rishi Panchami.

Sisters and mothers that day in the river attired themselves with similar clothes over different shades of skin. A short strip of a sari, a loincloth, or a shawl winded around them from their cleavage to the knees. I have no idea whether they intended to hide their gems but I could see everything through the thin lining of clothing, from top to bottom, right to left, and front to back. Everyone had their hills and plateaus at exactly the same places, valleys located between the hills precisely, and deep bushy Kali Gandaki gorge at their body's sagittal end. Some were desperately trying to hide their gems but they were gleaming bright with nonchalance to the rest of the world.

The women that day let go of those covert gems and put to display to Mother Nature alone which they had only doffed to their men. A strong bond of unspoken fervor bound these women no matter where they came from.

Names were different but stories were tied with similar threads of narratives. Rishi Panchami had befriended them despite they barely knew each other. Each woman found the other her own. Each saw in the other her self. Glad and gleaming at least for this day.

There were no males in that open-sky convent. A bit higher up toward the tree stop, there were children like me loitering around. They're like display mannequins. Their eyes were gorgeous.

Those who saw these women for the first time were astounded, perplexed, blown off, and were blushing at the glamorous river-side exhibition. Truly a woman's day it was. They're shouting at each other, often at the top of their lungs, mocking and cracking jokes. Their happiness had no skies; their lips opened wide, eyes constricted, teeth exposed. Some of them were brushing their teeth 365 times with Datiun twigs, once for each day of the year, according to the tradition. The adolescent girls who had menstruated of late and were inexperienced of the religious protocol were being guided by their seniors. A small group was scrub-cleaning their vagina 365 times. Few were immersing their body into the shallow waters for an instant. They brought up everything that was at the bottom. The rest were in the midst of these actions.

The women's countenances were facing the Narayani river opposite to each other. Some women flopped down on the sand out of uncontrolled bursts of laughter. They're giggling and passing vulgar comments on each other's bodies followed by snappy comebacks.

But women were not supposed to expose their private parts or talk about it, and even touch them with the sense of pleasure, as the society dictated. What a shame it was! However, there was no one to build those kinds of question-walls there; the walls had been broken for a while. Every single thing that was taught to them since their very first day on earth was differed until sunset. I'd seen the walls demolished with my own eyes. And more than me, the Narayani river had witnessed it.

If someone could relate to these women's destiny better, it was the Narayani river, who would have to do the same if she hadn't had the magic of that gushing drift: pick Datiun sticks and scrub it throughout her body like the rest to feel holy and clean. I wonder whether she'd have a different fate, a different story to tell. Like mine, all the same. I too wouldn't have any different story to tell than to think, wait for, and speak about this fate like the rest of these women. Or would I?

I doubt how this one-time-fits-all attitude does any good to women. What does it mean to you when you brush your teeth 365 times a day and that sufficed sanitation for a year, that you wipe-cleaned your vagina with red clay 365 times and it would be immaculate for the rest of the year?

And that with clay? Clay means germs. Germs in vagina is the recipe for disease, everyone should know. God knows what Book substantiates the cleaning of sensitive organs with river water which carries the filthiest of the filth with it. In it, actually. I don't find a rhythm between what I've studied in school and what's being done today in the river right in front of my eyes. Well, I've not read enough to tell the difference. But if river water was clean, why boil it to drink; why brush your teeth throughout the year if once is enough-isn't this common sense?

Around thirty minutes later, everything changed. The women finally finished off their river rites and peregrinated towards us. There was a variety of red-clad clay organs these women were wearing. Somewhere, the Kali Gandaki gorge had turned callistemon red, in some the valleys seemed to bear volcanoes, while in others the entire hills were spotted red like the perennial poppies of choice.

The women gradually encircled the resting spot in an act of involuntary coordination and reminded me of the hide-the-handkerchief game we used to play at school or when the teacher didn't want to teach because of cold and so we retired to the playground encircling him, enjoying the sun more than anything else. Unlike in school, these women circles had few males in them. Some of them were old men who knew-it-all. Some were young lads but confident, with yard-long dhoti wrapped around their waists and legs. They wore kurta on the top, and waistcoat over them with Dhaka garbed on their bald heads. These men took their places, their books of varying volumes, some under their armpits, and the rest opened up on the floor. The women were ready for the rite.

With my back displayed to the Narayani river, I saw and recognized the Panchami puja, a type of veneration menstruating women perform after cleasing their body in the river. There were adoscelescent girls eligible to come over and join for the ghaitopuja, a rite for the ones who had menstruated post-Panchami last year and pre-Panchami this year, that is, the menarcheal adolescents. They were so ashamed ants moving tirelessly on the ground and doing the Sishyphus triviality interested them more. They watched it with their faces turned red. One could easily recognize them because they had the earthen pot, different from the others.

Throughout the rite, the girls did not speak a word as if they'd accepted what fell on them, as would be told by their mothers. Good that they accepted their fate because they'd committed a crime, a blunder, and even more-a sin. Like my mother said.

We're sinners. I, you, alike.

When I was almost seven one morning, I asked my mother why the crevices of her legs were bleeding profusely. I was aghast at the spectre. The blood lines ran down her thighs like brake-failed taxis swirling downhill, only to meet with the ground. It was visible on lifting up the loincloth she'd wrapped around. I knew how it must have felt from the incident. When I cut my finger's tip with the brand new sickle father brought out of my desire to inaugurate it, I had almost wetted my nice blue skirt, pestered by pain. It persisted for almost a week. I couldn't stop discerning how diligent our hands and fingers were when we don't take notice of their functions. From wiping a damp, dirty butt and cleaning pots to washing clothes and eating, I realize the profundity of these tasks and the degree to which we take our hands for granted.

For exactly the same reason, I was worried what mother must have gone through leaking that amount of blood and that too from a difficult spot I knew nobody could easily cut through.

Mother was but as relaxed as a frog on a sunbath. She had no agony on her face, no sign of trouble. She stared on my eyes with her dead face and said, "I'm menstruating. I have been untouchable."

Okay, that went over my head. What menstruation? Who shunned her? From what?

"Your urinary organ bleeds. It happens to everyone. It'll happen to you too. Word has it that we're living the sin of some curse on the gods."

Who is everyone, I pondered in nervousness. I? Sister? Father? But I've never heard anything of them.

"Will I get it too, mother?" I demanded.

"Yes, yes. When its age, it happens to every women," mother lashed out at me as her words trotted, as if she's tired and bored.

My curiosity fueled my persistence.

Like an unstoppable train, I asked, "Will father have it? Why me? What about sister, is she going to have it?"

"What are you trying to say?" She symphatized at my question.

I was frightened to hear that I was cursed.

"A curse of gods? We bleed because of that?"

I never learned why gods were so angry at us, the female. Why would someone curse? For what?

When mother was on this 'menstruation', she didn't do much of the inside-house chores. She mostly stayed outside for five consecutive days with her own set of utensils for eating. She ate separate from us, washed her utensils, and wouldn't let them inside the house. She kept them nearby the rain porch and often I don't know where. There were also separate sets of clothes for her to wear and sleep on. She washed her clothes secretly before everyone in the family woke up and hung them to dry in places we didn't find. Mother disagreed to be part of any veneration or ritual nor she accepted eating any offering put to the deity. When father walked through the rain porch, she flew away of the fear of touching him, like a cat flees a dog. It felt strange when she didn't even touch any plants in the backyard. She didn't eat the fruits. Early in the morning of the fifth day, she took a bath and sprinkled holy water around herself. After sprinkling a bit of cow urine onto her, and before the village woke up, mother lined the uneven floor of the house with a paste of holy cow dung and water. This, she said, purifed the entire house of her menstrual sins. Her used clothes, the ones which dried easily, were rinsed with water and ashes, and the bulkier ones were made pure by sprinkling holy water from some religiously agreed-on, sancitified river. Without these things done, my mother would still be impure, unfit for doing and touching the utensils and chores. Unfit for touching anyone or anything, even my father.

I had this hunch that because women couldn't do usual tasks and were barred from participating in religious functions, they were said to be 'untouchable'. But the terminologies were different according to places and practice. Whether you say shunned, pushed off, untouchable, or sarcastically-Brahminized, holier-than-thou-ed, or priest-turned, it is similar in conduct-you're officially excommunicated from your family for few days like an outsider, every month, without having to regulate or enforce by any member of the family.

I do agree I digressed a bit, time- and thought-travelled to where it took me. At the river, the women were in a rite. The priest asked them whether they'd brought cow's urine with them called soon pani (literally: gold-water)-that when sprinkled onto someone cleaned all sins. The rest of the proceedings were so esoteric I didn't listen, couldn't make sense of them at all. It was partly because I was caught up with the preliminary roots of it and was completely lost in the illogicality and profundity of the task.

I tried to get my head around this so much I succedeed in grasping why the Panchami Puja was done.

The Rishi Panchami puja was a symbolic exorcism-cum-purification ritual to ride away all the sins women were cursed when they touched what's not allowed during their menstrual days. Mythology has it that in the Satya Yuga, in a place called Vidharva, a woman named Jaya Shree, wife of a man named Sumatranam, touched the forbidden objects and had to be born as a dog, and her husband, as an ox-to sanctify their sins. The priest told me this story.

I asked no one about this the second time. At least it was not the right place and the right time. I was just a teenager. I sat and waited for everything to wrap up. Until then, I questioned myself, and became satiated by my own answer.

No. I will never be in a ghaito puja. Even though mom told me I would bleed one day and I was a sinner, I never believed her. I was adamant that I wouldn't bleed, would do nothing that could cause me that.

Until that very day came when it happened to me the same way as to my mother, and millions of other women.

The holidays in Prembasti school, which I studied in, were to start the next day. That scorching afternoon as I returned home from school and headed eastward from Sitaram Chowk along the irrigation canal-road-I remember it was a Friday-the last at school for summer vacation, I felt an uncomfortable sensation under my skirt. It was a strange sensation, something tingling, as if a tiny monster sneaked in there.

I groped around in my lower front and back periphery but found nothing. My hips wore a home-made petticoat-like undergarment fastened in with a cotton drawstring which upon reaching home I investigated as soon as I rested the books on the rain porch. I needed to ascertain what crawled up through my vaginal pore. I squatted on the toilet floor and urinated in the hope that the thing will flush out. Deep clots of blood mixed with urine came out instead.

Told you. As every mothers would say.

So it was my time to bear the sin? I felt smothered while my world as I knew it changed in a day, the last day before the long summer vacation began. The beginning of the vacation aired an indelible impression in my psyche forever. I remembered what mother had told me earlier. It was for me a menacing apparition of horror that came to life and made me its substratum.

You're a sinner and so are all women.

Hitler Usha sister, what about her? When my parents were not home, she was the boss. If we do not play obedient at her behest, she'd not wait a second. Her hand. Our back. A bang. And a wail. It was clear nobody messed with her. But no worries, I was the most obedient sister.

I did not think twice in gathering my books, kept them at the edge of the staircase base, grabbed an old withered frock which I wore at home, wrapped things up, and set out to the gateway to flee home.

"Where do you think you're headed, huh?" Usha sister bellowed.

"Sister's home," I replied back. I don't know where it came from.

"Sister's?" she asked.

Neither I could hear her nor I wanted to. I never turned back even once, didn't wait for a second. Because I was obstinate to not sleep in the neighbour's shed. What mother told, the sisters followed and slept in a cow shed for several days the first instant they menstruated-all of them-the eldest, the second eldest, and the third-born, Usha didi. I had decided I wasn't going to join the parade of the dim stars in the sky which barely existed for the world.

By the time I realized I had not obeyed my sister's command, I had already exited the house premises. For the first time, I heard Usha didi's voice doppler-shifting towards low intensity which otherwise was always the opposite.

I didn't realize I had crossed all the prismatic-roofed houses, flat-billed shops, marshes, and a culvert assigned by a stream that I started seeing father-or maybe his shadow, and was so frightened. Is father supposed to see my face? But what has he got to do with all this? He is innocent. As if he knows who's menstruating. Maybe because there is always someone doing the chores, nobody cared who is secluded. Father only knew when sisters prepared to flee to avoid being seen, or while eating.

Father was not home much but I remembered those days when father cooked while mother got fenced off to becoming 'impure'.

I shouldn't show father my face. Evil might befall him.

But I don't fear this. I'm only concerned what he'll say on my walking off. I won't have an answer then. Without noticing men who could suddenly turn up to be him, I flew through the air like an airplane without a cockpit. As much as I feared father, I also feared his acquaintances who could recognize me as the old Mr. Paudel's daughter or more popularly, the milkman's daughter. They might keep me with them to return father's memento, me. That day, I used all my breath panting toward hyperventilation, all my muscles, and forced every inch of my body to escape my village and my fate.

Physiological senses were numbed. I no longer felt hunger or thirst. Muscles were barely tired. Lungs had trillions of breaths left for such a daredevil act. Human physiology is amusing. Hunger and thirst seemed only to bother a person when they had nothing to do than eat and drink.

I hate you, Usha didi. My parents are uneducated. They can't think what's rational. But you're an educated woman; how dare you do everything people tell you in the name of tradition? How dare you, Usha didi?

Sisters' Adversaries, and Mine

It was one week prior to winter holidays, three years ago, that Usha didi had her first menstruation. Only when her friends at school pointed out, she realized what had happened. Her skirt recorded patches of blood back there. Usha didi melted with shame, fear, and guilt. Her friends swarmed her around, braced, and escorted her home.

An abundance of maize and sesame grew nearby home in sharecropped lands. Forbidden from seeing the ridges of the house roof, and father and brother-the male members of the family, Usha didi sent for mother. The maize and sesame leaves breathed out hot air due to the sun scorching on their leaves. She felt hungry and tired. She was disgusted of her body as her clothes had turned sticky, stained with streaks of blood. Poor Usha didi, tormented, fell asleep.

When she woke, a jackal held a hen by its mouth and rested nearby. It was so frightened it sacrificed its delicious meal and darted toward the green. She now had a mute friend, dead and lying. The maggots squirmed on the hen's pregnant body which Usha didi befriended until the evening. It was a long evening and only ended when mother called her.

Usha! Ushaaa!

Didi burst into tears when she heard from mother. One moment she was annoyed with her. Next, what was her fault anyway, she thought. Neither mother was at home, nor have road to Saili didi's, home, without crossing our front yard.

It was not easy for mother to negotiate with Saili didi, our neighbor, whose only daughter already had menarche. It only takes once to persuade someone to hide their single daughter. Mother but had five daughters, and only daughters, before a son. Five times to persuade the neighbors to give her daughters shelter, while economically weak. She could not talk them into managing space for her menstruating daughter in a barn. Even if they'd agree, the vicinity had distant relatives who belonged to the same gotra (lineage), so technically they couldn't offer sister a space. The only possible stay for Usha didi had to be at Saili didi's. Her home was not just nearer but also comfortable for delivering sister food.

Saili didi's husband was a strict man who had a fiery temper, and was at times bossy. He was obviously not very happy with sister coming to take shelter at his home.

I learnt about all this when I was told to deliver her food the next day.

Mother's daily chores had no longer been the same. She woke up along with the rooster's cuck-a-doodle-do and then woke sister Usha up with rustling whispers. Her feet treaded to the tap gently to fetch water. Mother chose a place where Usha didi couldn't accidently touch the fruit trees and could stay away from the vegetables in the backyard. She asked her to take a bath daily, wash her clothes on her own in secrecy, and taught her the dos and the don'ts.

"God knows when these fifteen days will pass. Why was I born as a daughter? After giving birth to two elder sisters, mother should have adopted birth control before I was even born," Usha didi welled up. "At least she didn't have to desperately coax people into allowing a hide-out for her forbidden daughter. To hide from her father and brother. All I could do was listen to my parents' rebuke and say nothing. I either listened to them straight or pretended that a living being was listening."

Usha didi fidgeted.

Mother was always busy with her house chores. Works inside and outside home was quite laborious by every work and health standard. Someone had to be there for help but how?

Usha didi had made the tiny maize jungle a thoroughfare to her home backyard. She mowed grass all day and carried the blindingly large weight of grass on her head-so large she had to grope the house premises tip-toed, just literally and then go back to Saili didi's home the same way, fearing somebody would know.

"I had the opportunity to see my home, its roof-ridges, and its way back here. I felt happy just to have seen it. I hope everything is fine at home." Usha didi asked me out of curiosity, mostly, but happiness and fear at the same time.

I understood nothing, could do nothing, and so did nothing.

On the early morning of the fifteenth day of her menstruation, didi took a bath, cleansed herself, and appeared at the rain porch with her face hidden inside mother's headdress. Father gave her some akshatà, reddened paste of rice grains, and a piece of red cloth after which she was said to be cleansed.

I was paying heed to everyone's actions: who did and said what. Are these the same rites I was supposed to do when my time comes? And like this?

I pondered what girls whose fathers were dead would do. Why does it have to be father, and not mother or any female for that matter, who has to remove the 'shroud of shame' from the daughters' face? Do fathers really fall sick with the mere sight of their menstruating daughters? How did that really work? I had only known germs made us sick. But menstruating daughters? It was really a puzzle to me.

I watched the whole scene as a mere spectator. Throughout, Usha didi looked at the boring floor and I-her eyes. They were flooded.

I didn't quite ask nor understood why they need be. She must be joyous though at her homecoming and new clothes. And she must have been saddened at the sight of father. Bothered at the dramatics.

Again, why torment of such a scale to a daughter? I was determined to not be the part of this dramatics. I knew I wouldn't, but how couldn't I?

This, however, was not the first time I'd seen something like this. The entire scene was a repeat live-cast to me; what had happened to Bindu didi, second-born to my parents, happened to Usha didi.

Bindu didi was in class seven then. She had learnt about menstruation from her friends when she was in class six in Gauriganj school. There was no toilet in school. The stream dug through a private land at the school's posterior was the substitute. The boys used to excrete out on one side of the stream; girls would take the other.

Bindu didi had menstruated on the same stream while urinating. It was just a red-ish spot. She was puzzled whether to let parents know. It could be a leech, she thought. But leech wounds in winter were rare to come by. She should have thought.

"What if I tell my mother and the next month nothing happens? People are sure to question my character. But if I bleed in excess later? How do I manage if something happens to my father or brother or at home because of me?" It must have been impatient moment for Bindu didi.

Eventually she decided to tell her mother and packed her belongings towards Saili didi's home.

The barn there was filled with dried twigs. Someone made space enough for our skinny sister (as we'd call her) and spread the homespun blanket. Like Usha didi, she practiced all rituals she had to and came home the odd fifteenth day.

I was bombarded with a plethora of questions: Why do women menstruate? What if they don't? Why do we observe menstruation rites, the dos and the don'ts that trail a woman's journey until death? What if we don't? Why is everyone silent on this perturbing practice? What is the solution to this perturbation? Why did nobody speak of liberation? Did Sita and Bhrikuti ever menstruate? What might Indira Gandhi do during her menstruation? These women were known to me through my school day quiz contests.

Neither anyone asked me nor did I tell them about it. I lived with these questions. Each day there was someone who menstruated. Some bled at home, some at school, and others in the neighborhood. Each day the sun set, I regretted having been born as a daughter; I felt inferior and contemptible. How couldn't I be born as a son, the saint, and ended up as a sinner? These questions baffled me and ate my heart out.

I was fed up with life. Mother couldn't bear a son for five consecutive births and maybe that's why a neighboring old man told mother-when she was pregnant with the sixth-that she would go to hell. Well, she wouldn't now because the sixth was a son. I figured out sons had the ability to book or cancel registrations to heaven and hell.

Women bleed and hence are destined to be sinners, unfit for performing any rites for the dead ancestors. Rather than dying every moment for being born, how about I die once?

I turned mercurial even at petty things and snapped back at my parents and even the teachers. They only had to scorn or scold my friends, and I would go temperamental. I couldn't eat or sleep properly.

If I am to die, why should that take time to bear more pain, disdain, and abuse? I concluded that menstruation was in essence the root of all prejudices against women.

I left home without a plan or purpose. I chose the right path for the exit because the left had too dense settlement for anyone to not notice. I dared to walk past Chowraalichowk which was familiar as it was my way to school until Tharu village but couldn't walk a step ahead. I don't know why I couldn't make it through the jungle. I should have.

I returned back the same path past Kami Kanchha's home, darted into the maize field, and hid myself in them. Our maize fields were healthier and denser than the neighbor's. I prayed to God sitting among these maize thickets dejected and chanting that I must die. The repeated prayers ultimately lulled me to sleep.

I woke up to mother's voice summoning my name and realized I was not dead. The sun had already set. And it was not a dream. If it weren't for mother, I wouldn't go home. After all, she'd be the ultimate scolding-bag later if I wasn't to reach home. "Why didn't you search for her?" everyone would yell.

I could picture those crossbeams that roofed the kitchen which I was barred from seeing and picture my mother sitting at a corner-these came to my senses with a pinch of respect and a tinge of love. I wanted to be at home, not away.

I soothed myself and called Lachhu, our dog. Well, I tried but nothing came out of those sticky lips deprived of food and water. I tried again. "Lachhu…"

Lachhu rushed toward me and showed my path home. Neither did I want to speak to anyone, nor I had to. That day, I did what mother told me like a good kid.

I was sad I couldn't kill myself. Coward me! Thought I didn't do enough to die right. Resolute to find an easy way to die, I deferred for a better plan. Death, it seemed to me, was as hard as life.

Bindu didi was but overjoyed because she menstruated the next month again. She was a felicitous woman now.

She didn't have to worry about her character. She was acceptable for marriage. She was worthy of all of this!

We used to call Bindu didi skinny if she annoyed us. She was skinny, maybe due to several cycles of trudges between paternal and maternal home.

And then happiness again.

They hid Bindu didi only for seven days during her second menstruation. She was happy for not having to pass those days in maternal home in Sahilitaar, Lamjung district. She had seen enough of torment of her maternal aunts observing their cycles. It was horrible. Separate food in separate plates; separate clothes-rusty and time-worn; separate accommodation and no beds; and separate places to wash clothes far away from water sources.

A certain amount of work was put off to be done especially during the menstruation period. Carrying manure to fields, chopping woods, moving rocks, and others. It was rare for a daughter-in-law to eat regular appetizing meals and that too during menstruation. Rough food and tough work were the days!

What books taught me and what I felt about rich and poor, tears and smiles, and good and bad were not in cadence. Definitions in books worked for writers and differently to different people. What surrounds you and your thoughts determine how you're shaped. Behaviors form when you try to adapt to your environment. That is what we call development. And mine was shaping.

My maternal home had neither extra spare clothes to wear nor clean handkerchiefs, not even ragged pieces.

Water was scarce and soap was unknown. Many things that a woman needed were not there. So, my maternal aunts had to improvise and because of this, they became 'defiled' and 'sinful'.

The situation was slightly opportune here at home not because it was really convenient but because we extracted convenience out of inconvenience. Poor Bindu didi! Thank god father called her from there in time.

My father had a dream for her girls, a dream to sprinkle some light in his daughters' life. He had sent us to a school nearby home. Bindu didi-who had lived on father's dream and who I thought had might and wit: I was displeased with her. How could she-who could do all kinds of masculine and feminine works and with her stalwart body-fear to talk about menstruation? Why didn't she teach us? I thought she was fragile, not brave, not intelligent, because she couldn't answer these tough questions.

Binu didi readily accepted the granary in the barn, in Saili didi's home as her home for twenty-one consecutive days the first time she menstruated. As a first menstruation of the first child in the family in those days, the times were tough and people too, with strict parents.

She was in grade eight when she first menstruated. Like me, she was unknown to it. Unlike me, she figured the know-how somehow. She had seen students at Prembasti School hide some ragged pieces of cloths somewhere in the canal behind the school building. 'Why would they do that?' she thought. Her underwear was full of blood and she needed a good absorbent.

Our parents weren't so liberal the same as everyone's. Daughters, and that too school-going daughters, and above all from a poor family-what more was needed: not just the family, but also the society barged against us in full swing. Digressing from the rules was punishable by eviction-societal and maybe physical if weak and poor.

Binu Didi complained:

So, I'm barred from even watching my home's roof-ridges? And father? Not even any males? Am I really barred from touching the fruits and vegetables I grew? Dairy products that I prepare? Have I become that untouchable that I'm fenced in from attending marriages and gatherings? Don't touch the book? Don't go to school? Don't wear those clothes? Bring your own straw-mat. Avoid touching water. Don't do this. Don't do that.

"But I did it all Radha," didi said to me.

Not far from Saili didi, our neighbour's home, in the vicinities, there was a buffalo shed. And topped by it were two small rooms, bamboo-fenced. Onc of them was occupied by Budhe dai's family. Budhe dai was a Sharki by caste and his wife, Budhini didi, Damai. They belonged to Lamjung district, my maternal home's place. Since it was an inter-caste marriage, they had to flee the village and settle in an alien place. The other room was a barn where fodders for animals and boughs and twigs were stored.

"Secluded from my daily work, I made spacc for myself by pushing aside some dried twigs and sat at a corner of the barn. Each morning and evening, I stripped the maize cob of its corn kernels, and during the day I mowed grass," Binu didi said. "Everyone who came to this place asked about me. I was the eldest daughter of Lachhimipure, my father."

At home, a mere baby boy was born after five consecutive daughters in a row, my only youngest brother Kishor. Centuries will pass until he grows up, completes his education, and looks after the family. Daughters are meant to bid goodbye one day, anyway. You raise them only to see them prosper a stranger's home.

"The house owner, an old man, would mutter around at times. His words generally found their way out whenever there were guests at home," Binu didi continued.

"'She can't not touch everywhere. She touches this. She touches that. Told you not to touch the vegetables. Wetted my plants with bathwater and, lo, they're dead now. And the cucumber beginning to fruit is dead to the ground,' the neighbor said."

"In short, everything that didn't work was up to me. The buffalo didn't give enough milk. It was on me. Not enough butter churned. On me. Bad dreams. You name it. They said it was a busy home. But I wouldn't crawl myself out of my space when people visited. I simply didn't want to. In an attempt to kill every minute and second, I went nearly insane." This, my sister's story, could be mine in future. Every bit of it.

Didi went on: "Some people said that I was ready for my marriage. 'To menstruate is to signal that a woman is fit for marriage, ready to bear children.' Nature is strange. Cows low; buffaloes grunt; and goats bleat when they're ready for their males. And when girls are, they menstruate. Mute animals cry when they want it. And speaking women silently bleed deep down.'" The women gathered around got excited at the vulgarity. They would heat up the air with their silly and sensuous laughter. They were gay and full of vigor.

"My heart but pounded. Thoughts danced uncontrollably in mind, fearsome and humiliating. Body was petrified with a mysterious fear of being attacked by them. Hearts skipped their beats. They who rustled the leaves came in where I was. They really did; I'm sure. Turn by turn. I screamed. Soaked in sweat, I stood up and cried for help." I got chills while Binu didi explained.

"What happened, Binu?" A voice was heard in another room, Binu didi startled. When Mother came in for help, she became the same man who scared her last night. And it happened not once or twice, but repeatedly. "I came to my senses and tried to convince mother. It was just a week since I'd been home and I experienced my second menstruation. I didn't want to leave home," didi said.

It was rainy season. The maize fields painted the entire area green. Luffa, cowpeas, watermelon, sesame, and grasses were opportunely growing among the maize giants. The fields were so dense one could barely make it through. The vines put together could be made into a decent living space in the backyard.

Father used to sell buffalo milk. He woke up at four in the morning and carried milk to the markets at around six. At three in the afternoon, he'd be back and by eight in the evening, off to bed. Didi had to schedule her works during the menstrual days according to father's daily routine. She made sure she wasn't seen or crossed paths when father walked. It was good time to sleep in the porch or the shed after eight in the evening. She persisted throughout the days this way.

"It was an awful experience to sleep in the shed. I mistook the buffalo puffs for hissing, slithering snakes. Grasshoppers and worms wriggled over my body and at times found their way up to my head-holes. When dogs barked outside, I was frightened for things that might have happened. I couldn't sleep for long, not a moment at peace.

I rather dozed off in the shadow formed by the tall grass bundles during the day. It was so un-feeling," didi said.

My sister's stories kept on flashing on my mind as I walked on.

I retreated to the chinaberry tree's shade nearby the cottage at didi's home. I was reluctant to enter inside. There was no sign of movement except for the drying clothes waiving to and fro, welcoming me inside. I was weary and lacked the spirit, laughter, and joy which kept on tapering since I started off from Hakimchowk.

The courage with which I had avoided Usha didi's face and told her I was visiting Binu didi was no more. I didn't know what took me here and nowhere else. Was I so sure that they would let me in? I didn't know. I wheezed a bit.

I knew I shouldn't return back. I can't be that what my sisters were; I can't do what they did, at any cost. Mustering some courage, I pulled the bamboo bar-gate that kept the animals away with some intentional thud so didi and bhinaju (brother-in-law) would see me at the gate and had to welcome inside.

Didi came out. My eyes played hide-and-seek with hers. I wore the face of embarrassment. We stood together for a bit near the pillars.

"Have you come alone?" she asked, suspicious.

I nodded.

"Why would you?"

The ants were moving closer to didi's feet but couldn't climb on her slippers. There were many.

"Are father and mother okay?"

I nodded, again.

"What is this you've brought?"

The light pack of clothes made my heart heavy. Didi took it from me and untied them.

"So, you've come because of menses?"

I gestured with my head. My eyes waited to cry, like a child who'd lost her beloved mother.

Brother-in-law having heard everything came out of the house.

"Shall we go inside?" he said.

My tears were of delight. I didn't let them roll because I wanted everyone to be happy, especially didi. Brother-in-law approved my visit. I didn't have to live in buffalo shed anymore.

The Pursuit Continues

Pokhara Gate, Amarsingh town square.

Two rocky retaining walls, on both sides of the road that led from Amarsingh town square to Gandaki hospital square, accompanied me. The design on the walls took me back to the days when I made ashtrays out of black clay. I made different objects each time. My mind made different shapes but hands always ended up crafting Maachhikatlaa (fish-scales). The black road demarcated the retaining walls imbricated with these fish-scales. On the march through this road, with hungry stomach and fragile feet, I saw the flowers and foliage of poinsettia and bougainvillea sway on the right. Peeking through those flowers' lattice windows, I could see what I had come for:

Tribhuvan University,
Institute of Medicine,
Nursing Campus,
Ramghat, Pokhara

This was neither my expectation nor my dream. It was a mere benediction by chance. During the days when I had to fear whether they'll marry me young, I had this opportunity to go for higher studies. I was happy on hearing I could actually leave my home. I didn't whoop, just grinned with joy and overshadowed the feeling. Maybe, I cried.

Father assigned his daily milk delivery to someone for few days and headed for Pokhara. I had got into the merit list for Intermediate level in the Institute of Forestry where I discovered some boys of my village also studied. But father changed his mind and admitted me to a Nursing College instead. Someone had told him women could not patrol the forest, confront the illegal loggers, and fight with wild animals.

Fine. I can live with that. Now that I had made it-it was not a mere lottery; it had slowly become my dream.

I started dreaming day and night. I pictured the faces I might see: the students, teachers, and the class, remained preoccupied with them. The mere thought of moving out of home to an alien place petrified me, and I slept less every night.

It was not so long ago that I had been discharged from a hospital. Just five months. I was off to irrigate the fields and slipped into one of these barbed wires. It incised a deep wound on my leg and gave me a fever. I was rushed to the hospital and came to my senses only three days later. I mistook that evening for a morning.

It was a small, dark room. Father squeezed one of my buttocks. A lady dressed in white warned me to brace the impact and injected-Ouch! It was not my first time in the hospital. Back then, it was father who was admitted because of stomach ache. I had realized that the ladies attired in white apron, white cap, and white sari were called the nurses. When I saw them for the first time, I had questions on my mind. How come they not get tired? How could their hands, dexterous in domestic chores, handle injections, clean wounds, and deliver babies? Don't they feel shame, or shy away from doing all these? They must have attended hospital after mowing grass and collecting animal dung at home, like me. But do both with same hands? Eww!

I felt a strong stench of animal dung. My hands reeked of it when I smelt them. Never ever had I felt it: these were the same hands which devoured food after collecting animal dung. It seldom stank. Each meal I ate after the work, I gulped the taste of labor in a flash. I was happy though. No more dung work.

All things come to those who wait.

I was finally at the gate of the Nursing Campus.

"Do you have the admission slip? The gatekeeper interrogated. "What…are you here to become a nurse?" He had a voice like a foghorn.

My 'yes' of confidence at this gate was going to be years of pride. I nodded, as always. My inside voice, however, was loud and clear: 'If others can, why can't I? I can and I will. I will be a nurse. I will be like Florence Nightingale.'

Florence Nightingale was the lady who spent all day and night ferrying hope to the rooms of the wounded and making her life's motto to nurse them during the Crimea war. Tall lady, oblong, spotless face; hair with a clear parting-line; and with a lace cap that veiled only the back-half of her head-The Lady With a Lamp! I wonder how she mustered all the courage, vigor, and enthusiasm to serve the needy.

As I entered the gate, the path to the college bifurcated-one short and another long. Far into the distance were houses with their identical roofs aligned, on the top of which stood the magnificent Machhapuchhre Himal-the Fishtail Mountain. The machha-the fish, and its puchhar-the tail, also bifurcated, welcomed me and said ‘everything’s fine’.

Things will get in shape with time. Machhapuchhre Himal taught me. I tried to master its resilience and sing the song Machhapuchhre Himal sang:

When it snowed, I befriended it, learnt to stand undeterred. When the sun’s heat bellowed, I learned to melt, relax a bit. When it clouded, I played hide-and-seek with it. And whenever the golden rays of sun first inaugurated the sky, I learnt to blossom with radiance. I am omnipresent. My shadow stretches as far as the clear waters of Fewa lake. Whether for painter or litterateur, songsmith or businessman: I’m here and I’m there; I’m everywhere.

Just think about it. I’m a rock, after all. A giant black rock borne out of some turbulences below my feet. Born out of a random event. Just like you. Cheap and rugged-I know. But what’s in an appearance? My peak looks like a fish tail, and that’s why I’m so likeable. Naked inside, just cladded by some white. You only need few qualities to be likeable, you see. Don’t strive towards perfection of the whole. Strive towards polishing your fishtail. No matter how worldly the world is, you will get noticed.

I took the advice from Machhapuchhre Himal.

Oh! Machhapuchhre, I wandered lonely as a cloud. You got me grounded.

When I was in the hospital, I never felt alone. There was always someone in company. New patients, new nurses, new visitors, new bird outside the window, and new me. All these concocted, made me love this profession. I became more benevolent towards it because of their support and affinity. Head bowed day in and day out in reverence. Hands learnt delicacy and compassion. My confidence and commitment towards the profession surged all of a sudden. Every single object: tables, books, and even the floors were close to my heart. They were for me as reverent as nurses around; they, with Na.Kya.Pokhara engraved on their backs, felt like home.

Whenever I told people I was a nurse or a nursing student, they always took me or rather mistook me for a Sudeni (midwife) who assists childbirth.

"So, you a Sudeni?" they'd say.

Initially, I used to get angry at this. Well, Sudeni is not a bad thing to be per se, but my profession is much more than that. Yes, my profession includes midwifery and I assist women in delivering babies. I understood it when I started taking a course from our Campus Chief Laxmi Rai. It was a small class to the left of the library. Mrs. Rai looked like mother: short stature, fair complexion, short braided bun, and sleek, perfect pleats in the sari. Her voice, soft but shrill, garnered the attention of every students. Well, the secret lied in her eyes. When she taught, the class was so quiet I would hear my heat beat. It was back in 1990.

On a fine morning of 21st August, 1988, I remembered the moment when I tried killing myself and felt an unusual sensation in Mrs. Rai's class. The legs of the chair I sat in trembled. I checked into my friends' faces for inquiry but their eyes were fixed on madam's face like somebody statued them. As if they were reinforced into concrete. They were glued to their chair, and the chair glued to the ground.

It felt like an earthquake.

While the earth was shaking to its full, all I could do was repent my journey away from home seven years ago. I'm sorry, mother. I've only added trouble. I wanted to cry this out loud. My hands were joined together in an act of seeking forgiveness. I can't die without meeting you, mother. Not here, not now. Leaving home was a mistake. Each time I swallowed my saliva, the idea sank in deeper.

After a while, the mental earth-shake slowly tapered to a standstill. Nothing moved an inch, even though I was still feeling it. Mother must have forgiven me; I was not dead. Except for some chairs and stationery which moved here and their along with my friends' bodies-and which Mrs. Rai wouldn't like-everything was intact: the floor, the ceiling, the walls, and the building.

The incident left me with a question. Why did I remember mother first when I was about to die? I could have thought of something else. Like fleeing away through that open door. Or crawling under the table. What made me go back to my creator? The respect I had for mother grew by leaps and bounds. The anxiety attack became my vantage point and mother, the glorious spectacle at a distance.

Mothers are indeed special. They're the prime engines of this creative process. They're the creators. They're the species who can compress millions of evolutionary years in nine months. Every single human walking on this planet had her/his mother. And this creative process can have no beginning or end without menstruation. Menstruation is the Big Bang of the human universe!

Busted!

I learnt that:

The uterus is composed of three linings. Menstruation is associated with the inner lining. When this lining ruptures, it bleeds and is excreted out through the vagina. This is called menstruation. As girls enter adolescence, some of their hormones and chemicals spike, while others take a dive, due to which the inner layer of the uterus becomes thick, soft, and rich in blood vessels. If a sperm meets an egg, a baby is formed. In this case, menstruation stops and gives way to the development of the baby in the uterine wall-that usually takes nine months. In absence of sexual contact, because of some diseases, when a contraceptive is used, or as long as there's no meeting of a sperm and an egg, menstruation persists. The cycle of formation and rupture of the inner wall of uterus thus continues every month.

The period usually takes 28 days but ranges from 22–60 days depending on women's physical and psychological condition, weather, diet, and other factors. It starts in girls at an early age of 10–15, called menarche, and stops in the '50s, called menopause.

In absence of any blood- or sexually-transmitted diseases (STDs), or any contact between the blood and foreign objects like a menstrual cup, tampon, etc., menstrual blood is absolutely pure. It is entirely different in appearance and composition than that of the blood you expect from cuts and wounds. It's more dilute but still contains iron, hemoglobin, protein, cholesterol, bilirubin, and platelets like blood in other blood vessels.

Some women say their menstrual color is oil-like but it varies from women to women and according to the time and duration of menstruation. Early menstrual blood is pinkish and gradually turns into red, bright red, and to brown. The darker the color of menstrual blood, the longer it stayed in your uterus. For the same reason, the color of menstrual blood secreted after rest or sleep is also dark.

In absence of any ailments, about 30–80 ml of blood is lost during each period. If the endometrial lining is thick, more blood loss can be expected.

There are a plethora of menstrual myths prevalent in the society. The queen of all is whether menstrual blood is pure or impure. This conundrum is actually a definitional conundrum, not a factual one. The purity of menstrual blood has nothing to do with chemical definition of 'impureness' as constitution of impurities, or microbiological definition of 'purity' as absence of microbes. It has more to do with humanitarian definition of whether what brought you to this world is pure or impure? In fact, this is more an existential question than a definitional one.

How on earth can the blood which nourishes the baby for nine months be impure? The inner lining of uterus is a holy site for baby which takes human shape in nine months: how can this place where the menstrual blood originates be impure? Menstrual blood is as pure as the baby born, as pure as the baby's blood. It is the holy water, when sprinkled on the baby, his/her heart beats, organs function, and life in it instils. Menstrual blood is holy blood.

Society has, however, a different story to tell. I remember when my mother talked about it for the first time.

This is because of some god's curse. Menstrual blood is impure.

I suddenly lost my temper with mother. Actually, parents are the primary planters of the seeds of ignorance and sin. On the one hand, I have what the teacher taught me, and on the other, what my parents said. Is it fair that in the pursuit of truth, one always has to be disillusioned about the intellectuality of their parents? About how right or wrong they were? How they can't be right in everything they say or do? Father had to know more than mother. He was the one with all the exposures: been there, done that. But he couldn't be different than mother. This-I have held it against him, and rightly so. I don't understand what mechanism in his mind allowed him to send his daughters to school against the opposing society and at the same time consider them inferior to men?

I wanted to hurl myself to home.

I have too held it against innumerable fathers and mothers who didn't just trouble their daughters and discriminate them in the name of 'observing' menstruation but also instigated others in doing so: parents were the real villains. They were sinners.

A war was going on inside me, and it was burgeoning. With a heavy heart that convicted parents, neighbors, and society, I rushed toward my college hostel, and nothing, not even the alluring Machhapuchhre far off in the horizon, could entice me.

When I opened the door to the hostel with a heavy heart, I was welcomed by the great Parijat. She stood there, hung up on the front wall. Her book, With the Sleepless Mountain, was the first extra-curricular I had read. That too, Shanta had given, in confidence. Both the book and the author had shaped me in different ways. I had sketched Parijat with her half-veiled hair and slanted posture, eyes straight, in a white A6-sized X-ray film envelope some few months ago. I hung it at the spot where my eyes could meet it from every angle: from the front door, while sitting at the table, and from bed. I could hear her talking to me:

Radha, don't be a foolhardy. There's no point in losing your temper with your parents. They're not the ones to blame. They're merely the mirrors. What their parents and society fooled them to believe, they did, and did all by their heart. It was the time of servitude and they served their master-the society, well. They taught you what they learned. What they knew. What they were told. It couldn't have been otherwise given their time and situation. Being a society is all about give-and-take. I give what I get. I get what I give. The society is religious about traditions. Don't be fooled with the pawns.

And more, they didn't go to school like you. Actually, didn't have to. But they sent you to one. Because they knew it was indeed a privilege to have gone to a school. Now, it's your turn, Radha. When you know that Nepali society is superstitious and ignorant, when you've read it in books, you can't pretend to put all the blame on your parents.

I was exerted. Parijat knew a lot about me. I knew what she said was true. I asked forgiveness with my parents for being so ignorant. And I vowed that I would become an example by being my own example.

I Taught Menstruation To My Parents

Third day into summer vacation

Gauriganj, Bharatpur, Chitwan

I asked my parents to sit for a chat. Something's coming up, they expected. From my early childhood, I read out to my parents and illustrated the topics I felt strange by drawing them. They believed in a lot of things I said. Complied with them mostly. Last year when I had come home, I had demonstrated to my father in pictures how one gets tuberculosis and also mother why she breathes with difficulty during her asthma attack.

I grabbed a paper and drew a uterus straight out, without explanation.

"This is the outer lining. This one is the middle, and here's the inner lining that causes menstruation." I scribbled hard with a red pen in the inner lining.

It bled. They didn't see it coming until I was midway into the lecture. I had a pretty good idea of how a baby is born; ways to assist in its delivery; when their sexes are determined; and how a child survives miraculously inside and outside a mother's womb.

Mother hung on to my words for some reason. She was glued to the diagrams. Father, however, was infuriated.

"Nonsense! What are we supposed to do with these?" he said.

Trust me, I had been waiting for this moment. The didactic bubble I had put around myself burst and spilled everywhere.

"Why did you send us to school then? To learn this nonsense, right?"

I knew the answer. It was a repeat telecast I'd often hear.

Mother has her own story to tell regarding education. She gave me a sudden strange glance. God knows what it was-of anger? pride?

"I went to school to beat my ignorance, father. To teach others what I have learnt. To make my living easier, and to be a part of progressive society," I went on. "Isn't that the purpose of education?"

This was the first direct encounter, a real dialogue, with my father since after I had left home. I was an unstoppable train.

"This is what I do in school. I spent my entire second year doing this. If you run away from my truth that you've sent me to school for, feel ashamed and disgusted, who am I supposed to go tell?"

I went back to the paper and scribbled frantically, this time with pencil, and not only repeated the entire class on menstruation but also put them to the test, at the end.

“Is menstrual blood really impure? Is it a sin?”

I waited for their reaction.

Their heads nodded in unison, in acceptance.

“What can we do when everyone does the same?” Their voice trailed off in retreat.

I felt a certain surge of Schadenfreude in me, but I constrained it to prevent the decorum of the situation.

And the lecture continued:

In the opportune moments that followed, I explained them all that came out of me: the dos and the don’ts in menstruation, our role in making the change, in being the change we all want others to be.

The Floodgates Open

The following year's Dashain festival, I was home for a month. It was late September.

Usha didi, elder to me and born third to the family, was already married. I had been taking up many responsibilities, by my age-standard. The family was now reduced to five: father, mother, I, my younger sister Samjhana, and the youngest brother, Kishor. Binu, Bindu, and Usha didi, in the order of their birth, had gone to their husband's home.

Anyone passing by our home would stop by for small talk. Being the first ever student in the entire village to have left for technical, and moreover, higher education, I presume I was special.

Menstruating during festival is a nuisance. I was in a fix whether to enter and work in the kitchen by declaring I had menstruated or to keep mum about it. Lying wouldn't be proper, I thought, for two reasons: first-is it possible to get away hiding the ragged cloth pieces? How do I wash them? Where do I dry? Second-lying to your family for reasons you ought to fight for didn't make sense, and that would be equivalent to lying to myself.

I decided that I'd do the work by letting them know. I have convinced my parents to some degree. I should be able to pull this off.

But what if they protest?

It is festival time and when people see me abstaining from kitchen work and not participating in chopping goat loins, they'd know and talk about it.

Though I was a vegetarian, I couldn't let mother grind on in the kitchen-and especially during Dashain when an entire billy goat, chopped to pieces, would have to be cooked. I wanted to be a helping hand to her; I always have, especially during festive time. It was a tedious task, and mother, because of asthma, couldn't sustain longer in kitchen. Every year in Dashain, she had asthma attacks and fell ill. This way, festivals ended up in insipidity. Happiness came to a grinding halt.

"Mother, I'm discounted. What am I to do?" I murmured through the door towards the kitchen. 'Discounted' was a code I and mother shared for being restricted from kitchen because of menstruation. I tried to maintain the glee and vigor as if I was playing around.

I coined this word during those days when I had to be barred from home, was forced to stay, eat, and sleep separate from the family. When you are discounted, or rather when they discount you, the value, integrity, self-respect, love and care towards you, your education, diet, communication-everything is taken for granted. It is devalued.

"Just keep mum and take the lead in the kitchen," mother said.

I hadn't expected an easy approval from mother. I was guilty for underestimating her decisiveness. How easily do we underestimate our parents?

Without displaying an iota of change in my behavior, I entered the kitchen. I was her daughter who had not given up. I felt proud and regarded the rebellious, revolutionary kindle inside her highly.

The family members, engaged in meat chopping outside home in the front yard, were concerned about me.

"You seem to be bothered by the smoke, Radha. First-time in the kitchen and with wood pellets? Poor thing!"

It was indeed difficult for me. To be in a smoky kitchen with a runny nose is not the easiest of the tasks for a once-in-a-blue-moon assistant. Despite the warnings, I continued.

It was almost ten in the morning.

I was lingering in the tap feigning a towel-wash. I couldn't figure out why but there was not much feeling of pride inside me of being a woman. I felt restricted. As if my limbs were tied to a pole with shackles. I remember Rousseau say: a man is born free, but he is everywhere in chains." True. But it gets denser for a woman. A woman is either not born; if she is, 'makes' her family disgusted; and if frees herself from that, will be chained. Only that the chains are many: society, culture, marriage, and you need to spend a good deal of time to put an exhaustive list.

The auspicious moment predicted for tika was quarter past ten in the morning. Hindus put a reddened paste of rice grains, mica dust, and curd called tika on their foreheads. They visit their relatives for putting the tika on and seek benediction. Although there was no one in particular who visited us, we had to put the tika on. If not for us, for them to see. For the society. If they see you with bare-forehead during Dashain, they'll presume someone in your relatives was born or had died. So, you've got to do things for the society. Live for it, most of the times. I wonder how many people live their life for themselves and for how long.

Everything from tika to food offerings were ready. The only being that was not was me. Will they put a tika on my forehead-that was the to-be-or-not-to-be question for me. Should I go, should I not? Am I asking for more? Do I'm allowed in kitchen mean I'm allowed for tika? I hadn't heard anyone talking about this.

"Hey Radha!" mother called. "Leave whatever you're doing and come to us. Father's been here since ages."

Is that it? Am I to go for tika?

Yes, it is. I'm the eldest around here and they wouldn't offer tika to my brother and sister without me. But was she really calling me for this?

I didn't ask. I went straight into the room. Mother acted as if nothing had happened. And I had no intention to wake the devils. I had faith in her. She's trying to give me wings, although in secret, so I could fly without those chains on. It might mean nothing to the rest of the family, but that's the way mother shows love. She's making a nest for me where I could enjoy my rights of living a dignified life.

It was time. Father put the tika on my forehead. He didn't die all of a sudden from heart attack or anything.

Then, it was mother's turn. I couldn't look mother in her eyes. I received the tika and bowed down on her palms. That day, I secretly took an oath of allegiance to not let my trust, respect, love, and affection towards my mother wither. Not now, not ever. I and mother together, after 17 years of my birth, were able to shatter one of the most persistent chains associated with menstruation.

She didn't fall sick this Dashain. Nothing happened to my father and brother. And I was the happiest.

The Reddish-Brown Hobgoblins Became my Thesis Subject

It seemed obvious that since the day I taught menstruation to my parents, I had been more confident, and my morale had been boosted. I began bringing up menstruation issues deliberately among my nurse friends to poke and challenge them to speak upfront. Many of them didn't want to disclose whether their menstrual days were on. Maybe they were afraid of public shaming. As a hospital staff, I saw their menstrual belongings while drawing cotton, gauge, pads, or medicines from the drawers. They hid it from everybody else. One knew that they had been menstruating when they either didn't come for their hospitalized family member and in case they did, stayed far away from their bed. They sat far-flung throughout the visit and returned back. Others didn't bring anything to the ill. And they didn't touch or eat.

I didn't expect this attitude from my friends, and on top of that, health workers. They knew human body functions. They did science. I was frustrated that they were watering the superstitions. They said they didn't want to offend gods. And "that was culture."

I debated and quarreled with them in a lot of occasions. Who made this culture? Why would the gods be angry? Where's that written? It would be nice to see it.

Studying and getting good grades was far from being conscious about real problems out there, challenging the superstitions. To question and problematize the status quo was and is really a hard nut to crack. It is painless to take things for granted. Rationality and scientific reasoning really need effort. To take a pause against the things we take for granted requires you to be rebellious.

When the Rana Regime started in Nepal, the literacy rate was less than 1% in women. Even after so many years, there's little progress made. Though the numbers have gone up, the result hasn't much.

I was devastated at the attitude, temperament, and behavior of people who had dexterity in political, social, and governmental services and were from decent and well-cultured families. How do we uproot this superstition regarding menstruation? What campaigns do we need? Why don't my seniors speak about it? Isn't this a problem?

These questions intrigued me. I looked at women's faces in public places and wondered whether they were menstruating. In the queues, in college, and in the market-I watched how they looked. All faces were similar. Some of them menstruated for sure.

Menstruation for me had become an enigma: you and your female family members know the feeling, yet it was like air-it's there but nowhere to be seen. As if it had no existence in the public. A mere private phenomenon which was unworthy of disclosure and discussion.

Menstruating women didn't have any mark in their forehead, no sign whatsoever. Do women manage to go to their study or work places whilst on menstruation? How many of them do that? Except in few instances where women have to say they're menstruating or when they're 'exposed,' it was a mist.

How can we live with double standard? Is our consciousness split between these two lives? How is it possible to put a happy façade when one is going through a debilitating physiological change?

These questions were kites to me and I decided to chase them, do an extensive research on it. It changed my reluctant attitude towards Bachelors in Nursing. I decided to do it both because of fascination and fear of stigmatization. I decided to pursue it because of the fear of giving up what I believed in.

In 1997, I got admission into Nursing Campus in Maharajgunj, Kathmandu. Even though I was already enrolled as a graduate student in the Education department in Central Campus, I went back to Nursing.

It was a place-even in graduate studies-where matured women in their twenties competed for excellence. No less than a rat race. I was an odd bird. I saw no battles. Just did my job. We had different battles to fight. I couldn't make a strong rapport with my friends. They were east, and I was west. We were strange bedfellows.

***

My friends were busy choosing the topic for the thesis. They ran from library to library. They consulted the seniors and asked for their suggestions while studying their thesis and the way they wrote it.

I was untouched by any of these. Mostly because I neither had someone dear to supervise me nor I had close ties to any student leaders in the campus.

My thesis Politics of Transformation was considered a major digression from subject in the proposal viva. Its focus area was menstruation. I made some changes to the proposal and went back to my supervisor.

"This subject is neither too easy for an amateur researcher like you," my supervisor Sulochana Shrestha said, "nor you can query your subjects. It's too sensitive." She warned that nobody had attempted such a sensitive subject before. And that it was too difficult to collect data for this work. "It is too shy a topic for women to speak."

"Understood," I said and made her feel that I understood. But I didn't want to. It's a big failure to quit before even trying and failing. If I can't do this, I'll know in a month, I'll change the topic after the field visit and start working next summer vacation, I thought.

Somehow, I managed to get the thesis topic through the proposal evaluation body. It felt like I had completed the thesis itself. I agreed verbatim with my supervisor that it was indeed difficult to pursue the topic: theories were difficult to hunt, and equally, those willing to talk. But I was determined. My agency for the act was backed up by an unconscious will to revolt against agony, discrimination, and inequality. I wanted to learn the whats, ifs, and buts and shout out to the world that this was what you felt shy of.

My duty station was Gokarna Health post in the then Gokarna Village Development Committee, now part of Gokarneshwor municipality. It was residential work. Either personal or professional, it used to be scheduled. My friends who wanted better for me felt for me on the topic I had chosen. They suggested me to take it easy with the subject, choose something that was fast, easy, and amounted to better scores. I knew they didn't want me to suffer. But unlike them and my family members who went along with ease, I was willing to play against the tide.

I stuck on menstruation as my thesis subject and worked day and night. Four days after I joined the field, I started collecting data. Mornings, evenings, and holidays, I didn't spare any. My subjects for study were both literate and illiterate girls and women of age group fifteen to forty-five. Surveying the women and meeting them became the new normal. At their homes, on the way, and in the fields, I was willing to go wherever I found people willing to speak. I found one, she gave me the address of the other, and then other, and the research groomed.

It was only few years into Maoist rebellion and therefore we were stationed not so far from capital Kathmandu. To be a stranger and on top of that interview people was seen as a suspicious activity in the village. I couldn't afford to pay heed to such potential stakes when something much important was at stake for years. I began to question my respondents.

Does your back ache while doing light works? Any white discharge? Is it of fishy odor? Does it itch or burn?

Yes, was the answer from most of them. After conversing on reproductive problems and venereal diseases, I slowly progressed my questions towards menstruation. After much said and asked, they were now open to my questions.

They started giving away their secrets which they had never shared with family members or even in a nearby health post. The number of petticoats they changed, its frequency, where they washed and dried-they confided.

Then, other questions followed: what was your menarche like? How long were you secluded? What works did you avoid?

With both oral and written consent to confidential information, I took their photo with a Konika camera I had purchased with the money I saved from the anesthesia training in Bir Hospital. It was not a premium camera but it gave me good memories.

The images captured were pretty. But the account of their menstrual days was horrific. There were streaks of blood in ragged pieces of cloths, in torn pieces of sari and petticoat, and in torn edges of bedsheet. A half or a full meter of shabby garments was their locally made menstrual pad. One scruffy piece used by multiple women in a single month turn by turn. The same piece of cloth was used by mother/in-law, daughter/in-law, and sisters. They were obviously at a collective risk of severe bacterial and skin infections.

They washed and hid the cloth in the crevices of firewood stacks, sheds, or the granary early in the morning or after dark before any family members woke. The member who menstruated first knew the hiding place. She'd then get the job done, and plug at the same cranny after cleaning, followed by the other members. The story was no different than anyone's.

I was Speechless

The images of Western Nepal bombarded my eyes when I entered into the UNICEF building in the United Nations Office in Lalitpur. I felt I was home; the women in the frames were like my sisters.

A menstruating woman in a shed grabbed some rugged clothes and sat in a corner. She couldn't go home, touch or see any males, or eat in her kitchen. Milk, eggs, and meat, the most nutritious foods in the village, were forbidden. She had to stay away from touching the vegetables and fruits in the backyard. There was a long list of what she couldn't do. After reading the report, which was part of my thesis investigation, I was aghast.

This practice called Chhaupadi was still prevalent in Gauriganj, in Chitwan, back in my village. Just with different names. Women were simply called 'displaced', 'opted out', 'untouchable', 'dot-marked', 'blasphemed', 'brahminised', instead of menstruated. For the first offense, they were banished for twenty-one days, fifteen days for the second, and eleven or seven for the subsequent offenses to some corners of the house. But for women in some parts of western Nepal, they had to leave home for shed no matter what the season or condition. Each month you had to spend few days in the shed. The crime was similar: that women menstruated, and were now subject to societal and cultural discipline. The practice was similar throughout Nepal irrespective of the place women spend their time during menstruation.

I coursed searching for internet on the streets of Bagbazar in a desperate act of finding how things were outside home. The more I delved in menstruation systems, the more puzzled I was. The rationales were different; the nature of menstrual observation was different, but the disciplinary mechanism that made sure it existed in the first place was similar. Whether it's Asian countries like India, Pakistan, Bangladesh, or African ones like Kenya, Tanzania, Uganda, the problem was persistent everywhere.

Having studied Medical Sociology alongside where you were told that traditional harmful cultural practices associated with castes, region, religion, were social evils, I was shocked to know that it was everywhere irrespective of the geography. If so, why was it tagged like it happened only in the Western Nepal?

I kept on digging multiple sources and rang myself with questions. It never failed to prove the point that menstruation was a global practice irrespective of family, caste, occupation, religion, or geography. It was practiced around the world by millions of women.

When I completed my undergraduate in Nursing, I visited Western Nepal to see for myself what really was going on. There I discovered that not just during menstruation, but also during childbirth women were forced to leave their homes into Chhaupadi huts for eleven days. Chhaupadi was not just associated with menstruation, but was only part of it. A lot of voices raised talked intensively on childbirth-associated Chhaupadi problems. We've been talking less and less about menstruation-led Chhaupadis, leave alone kindling activism. What was in the conversation only scratched the surface.

We had been so determined to dismissing the absence of Chhaupadi in rest of the country and tag it to the Karnali or to Achham and Bajura districts that we concealed our hideous practices in the garb of accepted euphemisms and taken-for-granted phrases. We shooed away any criticism against it.

Whenever I tell them we have Chhaupadi and point to the barring of women in their menstrual days, they dismiss that annoyingly as if in an attempt of definitional courtesy. "That's Chhuipratha (touch-barring practice), and it's different," they say. The entire emphasis was the type of roof women were allowed in during menstruation.

Giving an alien name to a thing similar in nature doesn't make it different from it much like calling a spade a bed doesn't make it a bed. That-women in Achham live in separate huts or shed and that of Karnali live in the ground floor of their thatched home obviously because it snowed-doesn't make them any different. Where people rear animals, they have to stay with the animals in the shed. This weakens winter as an excuse.

This was menstruation and that was not. This is chhui-practice (touch-barring practice) and that's Chhaupadi. The gravest of the issues that torment the world are not the issues themselves but the definitional battles that cripple their meaning and significance.

Goma Bhauju of Jumla

On 14 November, 2002, because of Maoists' attack in Khalanga, I felt I had been reborn. After I completed Bachelors in Nursing, I went to my dreamland Jumla where I met Goma bhauju (an elder male is addressed as daju-brother, and thus his wife, bhauju), a local businesswoman. The land compounded her home firmly leaving no spaces for kitchen garden and cattle. If at all, there was a toilet and a small space for bathing. The house had a kitchen attached to a large hall where her customers ate snacks and food.

Bhauju sat nearby Aji (her mother who was a Newar by caste) and took the propitious moment to complain.

"They don't let menstruators touch the pillars of the house. Only after cleansing the head on the fifth day, we're allowed to enter or touch anything. If we digress, Aji's body would tremble as if caught by spirit. Even my brother's. Our god is strict."

I had no idea that people could go to such ends in practicing superstitions, to the extent of delusion. I smiled but hid tons of historical agony inside. Whom to expect of minimal rationality and decency? From well-dressed, educated, or the witch-doctors? Or from doctors and nurses? The story is similar for all people irrespective of qualification.

Whenever Bhauju and Aji had some time to spare, especially when Bhauju menstruated, there'd be a squabble over who was mighty and modern and who was orthodox.

And we knew who was who. Both were orthodox just at different scales.

We sat around fire and talked about menstruation, motherhood, postpartum, citizenship issues, and some trivial stuff. They were always all ears to me and asked questions in between. Kids seemed to be the most interested; every time we spoke, they titled their heads towards the speaker and then nodded.

One particular evening, when we were together, I asked the children where the Devi (goddess) temples were. I pretended to know the whereabouts of Chandannàth and Bhairavanàth temples but not of Goddesses. The children flew their hands swiftly from their squatted position towards different directions, all at the same time, and bickered for a while.

"How many days in a week does the temple remain closed?" I asked.

They looked at each other to share their confusion.

"Never," a four-year-old boy said.

"Are temples supposed to close like schools?" The boy laughed.

Kabita asked, "Isn't Devi a woman, fupu?"

"Yes, why not. Gods are men and Goddesses are women." A man sitting around said.

"So, eh? Are they humans?" Another voice participated.

"They aren't different. If not, why are they called husbands and wives?"

Before the spark of the spat turned into a wrangle, I stepped in. "I wonder why goddesses allow people in temples during their menstruation days."

I knew that'd kill the discussion. But more than that, "it's time to eat" did.

Goma Bhauju ate outside separate from other members. I thought she was tired. But I discovered later that she had menstruated. She had planned to spend the night in the open sky, without my knowledge. I didn't allow that.

"If you're going to sleep outside," I said, determined, "I'm going to sleep alongside you for the next four days."

The yes-no give-and-take went for a while and as usual, I won.

She took her bedding and headed to the hotel's dining room inside, made her bed by joining benches. And I went to my room. It was a first-in-her-lifetime experience.

I usually did not disclose when I menstruated in Aji's family during the first few visits. After all, I was not regular. But when I did, I teased Aji by touching everything and often declared that it was my first day. Now, start shivering to exorcise this all! The next day Aji complained that she had developed headaches and a bit of toothache. I felt sorry for her and took the medicine out of the pocket. The mere sight of paracetamol on my palm would be the perfect placebo for her. Let's wait for a couple of minutes more. I'm sure it'll wane," I said. Whenever I visited this house, I felt the more I shattered Aji's superstitions, the faster she waned from them, through these experiments. After all, she got so used to it that her body no longer ached or shaked.

Something similar happened next month. Goma bhauju persisted that she could not obey what had been women's destiny for centuries. And I told her I could not let her continue like that; I pulled another bench, joined it with hers, and reclined alongside. She could fight me no more and finally gave up. We shared a bed together in the room which was just above the kitchen. Gradually, Goma bhauju did all the outside chores. Her clothes and countenance never showed that she had menstruated.

Those were the days during which Nepal Television had started its early few-hours transmission. In an attempt of gratitude, the home owner dai invited me to watch the TV. Goma bhauju couldn't come because she had menstruated. And I said I couldn't accept the invitation without her in the room. After all, I was no different and 'pure' since I had been with bhauju all along during her menstruation.

It must have been a difficult time for the landlord dai to perpetually fight over something that's completely illogical. He gave up. "Okay, okay. Both of you can come. Just sit nearby the door without touching anything."

The room inside had a black-and-white television with a shred of cloth atop. Dai sat on the bed and we stayed slightly afar. While I wasn't so excited about the room's wooden cabinets, there was nothing left to touch. He had to accept it because, as usual, it was a tried-and-tested consequence. However, because I didn't want children of that home to sense the conflict and Aji's god to get the opportunity to test his wrath, I would take things slow and wouldn't cross big lines, although I'd do it gradually.

Whenever women visited the hotel for its delicious momo, I pondered whether they're doing so out of hunger or because they couldn't go into their kitchen. These women touched everything in the hotel because nothing in their forehead said that at least one of them had menstruated.

Do women pilots cancel their flights when they menstruate? What about women chefs? Do they not enter their office during their menstrual days? And hundreds of women in government services-do they deny the service seekers from service? Do the service seekers ask whether they're 'eligible' to do their task? Of course not.

It isn't so hard to imagine why people fall ill (sometimes) when a menstruating woman touches them. Part of the reason might be what's called the nocebo effect (the negative placebo effect). If you're told, and convincingly, that something would turn out to be bad, the power of suggestion sometimes works so effectively that it might end up causing the malady. The nocebo effect works and several randomized control trials have proved it. In countries where the law mandates doctors and health professionals to inform their patients of the side effects of a medical treatment, there's always been a catch-22 on whether to do so. If you tell your patients about the possible negative outcomes, they might internalize it and the nocebo effect might work. If not, they might face charges against it. That is one of the reasons why only those people who are orthodoxical about the harmful effects of menstruation experience them. Those people who're educated about it, never.

As I visited Jumla and stayed there, I always said that I menstruated. Especially when Aji was around. One day when she had enough, she said Radha had become menopausal much earlier. Everybody giggled.

***

A time came when I was more frustrated of the people of my profession. She was a senior nurse of Jumla district hospital: I decided to visit her because she was gravely ill. Fifteen years ago, she had travelled to Pokhara from Jumla for her nursing study. She belonged to a dynasty-like family. Rich. Both of her parents and in-laws were from well-to-do and bustling places.

I visited her one day when her husband told me she was not doing well. She lied at a corner, body sweltering with high fever. Doctors were hard to come by; that might be the reason they were expecting me to visit. I took her vitals. Temperature 103°F, pressure 90/60, and pulse 55. She looked drained and pale. I suggested, as usual, to consume plenty of milk products and vegetables. She kept silent the entire time.

I felt awkward. Why wouldn't she talk? Did I say something wrong? I guess not.

Then she broke silence.

"I have menstruated. How do I consume milk and vegetables?"

"If you're doing this, what can we expect from the others? It was only last week that you gave a training on Chhaupadi myths, isn't it?" I couldn't believe my ears.

I remained for a moment.

"You're a sinner," I said to her.

A highly religious woman, she spoke in a trembling voice. "I don't believe in such things but I don't want to offend others. So, I stay away."

***

Same with new nurses. Back in 2016, while I was going back to my home from canteen at around ten at night in the B.P. Koirala Institute of Health Sciences' Dharan premise, I was followed by a group of girls. I was suspicious of their intent. Since I had never encountered with incidences of theft or robbery, I was frightened if it was more serious than that. After all, fear conjures up things that are least likely.

They turned out to be curious nursing students who wanted to ask questions. Not stupid questions, funny though. But could seem so on first encounter.

"Didi, may we ask something if you don't mind?" one of them said.

"No problem. Go on." I was curious.

"Do you go to Pashupatinath temple on menstruation? And worship there?" Two of them asked taking turns.

I laughed. "Do you know that I've religiously mourned my mother's death? Why would you think I wouldn't?"

They talked amongst themselves. Some of them believed me; some were reluctant.

"Listen. I don't tell lies. If I could, I'd become a politician," I said.

They shared the laughter.

A shrill voice from the group declared: "I know this is superstition. I'm a student of science. But I still fear worshipping or going to the temple. It is even stricter at home. Only that we don't sleep in sheds, otherwise we observe everything."

We talked for a while and parted.

***

The next day I gave a group of health workers a task: to sketch their house vicinities as detailed as possible. The next fifteen minutes they put in the task brought laughter, amusement, and often silence.

"Look at my house," one of them giggled.

"Better than yours," another said.

"I can't draw a house," the voice in the last row said, pushing her lower lip against the upper.

The answers to the questions were interesting:

3-8 rooms in the house.

1-2 Kitchens.

Toilet inside/outside the house.

Clothes dried inside/outside the house.

Stay home all day/go as far as to work during menstruation.

“It’s good,” I said to one of the drawings. They guffawed.

I was typically amused by a house which had a menstruation room in the second floor. Two beds were laid, separate from each other, demarcated by an empty floor at the center. The beds were non-identical-one of them fine-tuned in its wood-work, and the other, tattered. In the other picture, small strips of clothes were divorced to a place far off from home, from long-sleeved affluent clothes. Another picture had the clothes inside the shed among the animals. The most-privileged makeshift menstruation room was that in a multi-star hotel room. It filled the paper.

What was in picture was inside people. Menstruation was that practice which neither money could corrupt nor power could dissuade. Not even education could cleanse.

It was the incredible, the indestructible.

The Story of Hide-and-Seek

Wow! What does this funnel do?

Another lady said: "Does this fit inside?"

The next one: "Have you used it?"

I framed one answer for all of them: "This is designed keeping in mind things that we insert inside. It's called a menstrual cup. But I've never used it though," I said.

This was a discussion held in the office of Mina Kumari Lama, the deputy mayor of Hetauda Sub-Metropolitan city. While we discussed the gender-friendly programs the city conducted, Lama held a book Dignified Menstruation: Everyone's Business I gifted and said: "We've decided to work on this too. The budget is allocated. We've heard some boxes-like items for that."

It would be exactly what I was waiting for.

"I have all items. Give me a minute. I'll show it to you." I had darted through to the corner of the room where I had kept my bag, pulled the cups out, and displayed to them.

While Mrs. Lama greeted the people seated in a sofa towards her right, I placed all the menstrual items on her table as if displayed for sale in Ratnapark street pavements. I showed them pads sold in the market that wouldn't degrade in 200 to 1000 years.

Nobody in the room was interested. Not even when I showed them the 'magic' pad that degraded like a leaf. But the tampon elicited a reaction from them. They were amazed.

"Fine. This is easy to wear. It doesn't hang out like a blob from outside. The lady players use it. They don't complain that they menstruated in the midst of the game. It's slightly expensive but works straight for six hours. It doesn't degrade easy and even if it does, in a long time. Worse, sometimes we don't realize that it's still in there. Sometimes the thread would break off and if unlucky, toxic syndrome shock is easy to catch," I said. "It was I who two years back on the second day of my menstruation had forgotten the tampon inside. I remembered it at ten in the evening and was terrified by the idea." The others listened.

The chattering room was now silent. When I held the cup, everyone looked at me like children before magic show. I showed the room cups of different sizes and shapes. Cups of different brands, menstrual cups. Cups that lasted for ten hours and cups that worked for ten years. They were expensive but were now common in Nepal.

The deputy-mayor shot a question. "How come a single cup last for ten years?"

"It does. It's made of silicon. If you have a clean toilet or bathroom with clean water, you can clean it up without a problem," I added. "When it's time, go to the bathroom, take the cup out, and pour the blood collected in the cup onto the toilet pan or commode. Wash it clean and get it back in there."

The audience still watched in amazement. They were taking turns inspecting the cups, snatching from their peers. The deputy mayor grinned with her hand on her cheek. She looked rejuvenated.

I knew how the cup worked; it is now five years since I have it in my hand. I had a taste of every other menstrual product except for the cup. I can't convince myself well enough to use it. I often ponder how lucky I am to be able to use any product that's at my disposal unlike the vast majority of others who haven't even heard of it.

I should give the cup a try, I often thought. When I become menopausal, nothing matters anymore then. A person whose diet and work environment are unpredictable is likely to experience an early menopause. I decided I should use it next month. And then I decided the same again next month. That day never came.

I knew my cervix is relatively nearer to my vagina and required a small cup. Neither it is extremely hazardous nor bothering, I knew. But something has kept me from using it. On the first day of my cycle, I didn't even touch it.

I used to wear menstrual panties which I felt was quite comfortable. I had learnt about it since the last two years but hadn't experienced how it felt like until one day. It was some date, March 2018. I got the opportunity to meet with the director of a company, Madam Diana, in Brussels. I had gifted her my translated book Jumla: A Nurse's Story.

She gave me menstrual panties and some cloth pieces.

Diana was a Latin American management student. When she had gone to Africa to work in a bank, she had noticed on her way that the number of girls going to work were far less than the boys. She was upset by this random detail, left her job, advanced her studies and got into business. Temperament and determination help, it shows. But the majority of us live by without being skeptical to the daily experiences. We tend to sideline the whys and the hows let alone inspect the short- and the long-term effects. The westerners investigate on the same 'trivial' issues that are common sense to us. That ends up being an innovation.

Now menstrual panty was an entirely different story. When blood leaked into these panties, the surfaces of contact between the groins having the bifold made into a pouch that absorbed it. One had to keep a short handkerchief-size fluffy cloth piece in the gap, inside or outside whichever was convenient. It worked wonders for four hours. The only catch is you needed to wash it time and again. But it felt comfortable.

The panties are not new to me or any Nepali women. Those whose panties leak due to overflow during a sudden menstrual surge improvise with their friends' or family members' handkerchiefs. But the handkerchiefs are not so fluffy. They are rugged. Girls and women in Rolpa district usually use large, thin, colored cotton head-bands used for headaches. That way, a lot less people would know that women were playing hide-and-seek with the reddened cloth. Sometimes, as funny as it sounds, grandpas and grandmas without enquiring, use those bands for headaches. They say that relieves their headache a lot. It was ironical but true.

The material I had used before panties was a tampon. I had known and learnt about it as late as during my post-graduate thesis work. I used it for my rescue only in May of 2016.

Here's a story that glued to my mind and will ever remain. I was back from my field work in Kathmandu. After a strenuous series of work, my mind could no longer hurl my body to work, so I thought I'd rest. The next morning, I discovered I had menstruated. The first thing that came to my mind was the tampon. I pushed myself for the adventure. After all, I had nowhere to go, stay at home all day. It had been on my mind since a year and it had been so difficult for me to pull this thing off. Inge, my Austrian friend, had briefed all the know-hows of the act but I was still reluctant. She had even given a small-sized tampon to jumpstart my tampon journey.

I finally decided to resolve the long-held issue.

And what did I do? Kept the tampon in the drawer and locked it up for good. Like the cup. It was just more than a year of this hide-and-seek.

"I can't do it." I said each time Inge asked. "I'm afraid I might develop a real phobia toward it."

It can't go on anymore any longer, I decided. I inserted it inside my vagina and snug it tight by pulling my panties up. It felt uncomfortable. Like a wooden cork poking me at regular intervals. Does it always feel like this? How do girl swimmers concentrate without being conscious of their tampon? Earlier, I could not fancy the idea of wearing a tampon. Now, I couldn't sit with one without pain. Something down there continuously gave me a sensation of post-surgical awareness. I tried it twice. It didn't work. Maybe I didn't do it right. Maybe it's not made for me. It simply doesn't have to.

Farewell to Mahashankar Meetbà

When we started in this mission of activism against menstrual discrimination, we noticed that the biggest hurdle in bringing the change was the classificatory tropes people were divided into. Because of this, we couldn't fight against it as one species: humans. You're one caste; I'm another. You're rich; I'm poor. You're a male; I'm female. You're elder; I'm younger. You're one religion; I'm another. You're this, I'm that. Because you're this, I can't be this.

This doesn't mean everyone has to be the same. But it also doesn't mean everyone has to be different, every time.

So, we decided that anyone who got involved in the cause would unify themselves in this relation called Miteri relation. Miteri relation is as historical and as untainted as the relation of Krishna and Sudhàma in the epic story of Màhàbhàrata. When you consider another person as meet, you transcend his/her caste, creed, gender, religion, class, and geography, and associate oneself only with one identity: human being. Human being and nothing else. Miteri tradition is one such method of transcendence explained in the eastern philosophy which transcends human beings from their constricted cocoons of artificial tropes into the universal realm of humanity, based on mutual respect, trust, harmony, and co-existence.

Each one of us in this mission is meet to each other. Meetbà, meetàmà, meetdai, meetbhài and so on. Mahashankar Devkota was one such father-figure to all of us. And more than Nepalis, my foreigner friends cherished him.

It was Saturday afternoon. As usual, I was googling in my phone with occasional clicks through Facebook. The first news on the feed showed the dead body of Mahashankar meetbà (meet-vowed friendship, bà-father). Mahashankar Devkota, our meetbà, was no more.

His dead body was kept in the Nepal Academy Hall. The notice said the funeral rituals were to be conducted on the same day. I was heartbroken to have failed to meet him even once before death. More than that, I was saddened because nobody notified me about the incident.

He was in Nepalgunj about two weeks ago. All those days came to my memories like my father would say about him, the kind of person he was.

I had been to Jumla last Dashain with Inge and we both knew we had to visit Mahashankar meetbà. If he knew we left without seeing him, he wouldn't see us again. And if he didn't know, we couldn't not leave the place without listening to his articulate deliberations.

Meetbà hadn't talked much the last time we met. He hacked for minutes gasping for air though with composure. When he had enough air to breathe, with his books and certificates on hand, he pointed towards me and said, "Would you keep these in Shanti Batika for me, dear?"

I nodded to say yes.

A man often found in the kitchen, this time he was found lying on the bed. Under him, the puckered bed sheets distorted the image of bright electric-blue roses. He was surrounded by pictures of gods and goddesses, idols, medals, and certificates. An impromptu poet, he sat on the bed and recited poems and hymns instantly on the subjects being discussed. He was the first Deuda singer in Radio Nepal. But maybe because he was from Karnali region or didn't represent the right party, he didn't get deserved recognition. In 2012, when I made a documentary for UNDP N-Peace award, I had mentioned briefly about his work.

As usual, I briefed him why I had come to visit. Inge was menstruating. We shouldered with Meetbà squeezing him from sides. That was how we took photos. He loved clicking pictures. And he loved it more with foreigners. He talked impatiently with them while with great enthusiasm in his face. This time, he had been visited by a foreigner who could speak well in Nepali. But he didn't show much enthusiasm in talking. He just couldn't. His wife, mother as we would call, brought tea to his bed.

Mahashankar Meetbà was a deeply religious man, yet non-conservative. I would often visit him with a friend dalit (so-called lower caste) in caste. Each time he hosted us, he fed us well without asking my friend's caste. He didn't believe in stupid things that didn't matter. I was known to him as a person who'd been on a mission to abolish unfair menstruation practices in the name of rituals.

"Do not give up, success will be around," he said.

I always wondered what would happen after his death: would our relation tied by a feeble thread survive the utter materialism? That day had come, but I couldn't think of any answer except I would always remember him like my father figure.

"I can't talk today. I'm sorry," he'd told me-it was Dashain time. It broke my heart when I recalled the last visit.

His death was the truth. No matter how I tried to convince myself, I couldn't sit there and watch his photo. It was my last chance to see him in person, though dead. I decided to go.

I got rid of the tampon-thank god-and used normal commercial pad before I headed towards Nepal Academy.

There were many familiar faces there. From Tourism minister to different party cadres, people had come to see him for the last time. I was not amazed by the number of people he had earned. His sons, still in Jumla, were expected to come anytime during the day and start the final rites of his death. I met his daughters. We talked about him in a way we never talked about anybody.

His dead body had been loaded in a van to take him to Aryaghat, the place near which the electric crematorium was set. I sat along with others in the van. When his close family members observed the rituals, I did the same. It was going to be my first experience seeing a dead body burn in an electric furnace.

The bamboo casket he was on was taken upstairs toward the room where his dead body would be adorned and worshiped during the cremation. Then, he would be given the first fire by his sons and sent to the machine. There, however, no one except his own children were allowed. His sons took him into the room. No female members followed, not even his unmarried daughter, who was a nurse, by the way. Without asking anyone-and I knew it was inappropriate to ask; everyone knew it wasn't allowed and no one wanted to be either heroic or repentant-I decided to enter ignoring possible questions of why a distant daughter of a befriended man should enter while there were already his own people.

I pushed myself through the gathering in the gate. "Who're you?" the gatekeeper said. "Only family is allowed."

It was uncommon for him to think that daughters are not family because meetba's sons were inside and they were the only ones whom the priest needed to complete the ritual.

"I'm a daughter. I am family," I said, and I said with pride.

The gatekeepers said nothing. I entered. His sons were busy following the directions of the priest. I helped them in lightening the incense sticks and giving them items required for the cremation ritual. I saw his emotionless face lying there, prepared to be perished. Before meetbà was fed into the machine, I bowed touching his body, and left without a word, facing no one.

Pad-politics

The tampon must have waited for this day for me to even consider it using. It was quite unsuccessful though. I asked Inge what could cause such pain, whether it's natural or it was just me. "That's because of lack of skill. You might have placed it outside," she said. "But little pain during the first insertion is warranted. After that, you don't even know it's there. It has happened to me more than once. These days, I prefer cups to tampon."

I admit that it was placed wrong. I tried it once more and with might and left it there to test how it feels on usual works.

The tampon was a nuisance to me the first day. It constantly reminded me with its pricking sensation that it was there. But then it started disappearing from my mind and the awkward sensation was gone. I found tampon much convenient compared to menstrual pads when it comes to physical exertion. The only problem was its disposal. It was as much environment non-friendly as pads are. More than that, it's costly.

I preferred pads more those days. Admittedly, what's found in the market dominated what ought to be used but it was only one brand which lasted for five hours straight without worries. It was costlier than other pads and was not found in every retail stores. Unlike other pads, with which I did not have so delightful experience because of side-leaks and unwanted 'exhibitions,' for me, it was the best fit.

But others had different stories to tell. It all boils down to subjective experience. There are more than thirty brands of pads in the market; however, their quality varies widely depending on the cost and nature of material they're made of.

Pads for me are like handkerchiefs. We don't need one every time; but when we need it, we need it badly. It has been ages since I carry at least one such pad in my bag. It comes in handy not just for personal use, but also for others who are in real trouble. And we know the level of trouble one can be in.

That said, the use of pads also comes with side effects. I often had itchy and painful red sores in my groins. They're allergies. I had read somewhere that pads contain carcinogenic agents. Therefore, biodegradable pads are safer in comparison if the durability is not to be accounted for.

The ability of a pad to retain blood and prevent leakage is not the only feature we have to look for. One such important feature is its lifespan-the time it takes to decompose, or whether it decomposes in the first place. At the rate girls and women are using non-biodegradable pads, the earth will be a heap of pads in the future because of its 200-1000 years decomposition time. Moreover, in countries like ours where there is no check on plastic manufacturing, we don't yet have a safe method to manage plastic products like menstrual pads.

Pads are everywhere. Whether in highways or hotels, schools or jungles, they are the inevitable members of the garbage pile. Often a times, dogs are seen transporting and playing with them. Sometimes, the wind turns them into some fancy child-fan made out of paper or leaf and forms a twister. Pads have sealed the toilet pans in hotels and hostels and turned out to be a nuisance leading to increased expenses in unblocking them.

I remember one incident back in mid-July 2018, in Swargadwari temple in Pyunthan, when I had been with my father. I thought temple's toilets were generally cleaner than a highway-hotel's, and so I decided to use it. No sooner had I pushed the door, a pad at the doorstep welcomed me with its inside exposed to the air. In the midst of the strong urge to urinate, I captured it with my camera which I admit could have done after doing the job.

There are many schools which distribute pads to girls especially during the exams. I don't fancy this idea very much. To favor one menstrual item over the other is also a denial of human right of its own kind. Girls have the right to learn about all the products and be able to choose the right kind depending on convenience and affordability. When it comes to pads, we have to make sure whether a girl's or woman's right to a dignified life is guaranteed to validate its usage. The government should distribute pads free of cost or at least at lower costs, evaluating the prospects of all parties involved. Scotland distributes menstrual pads free of cost and India doesn't add tax to the products. We levy 13% extra on them.

We live in a country where handful of condoms are free but each menstrual pad demands a huge sum of money stripping girls of their pocket money and adding financial burden to the family. Why can't menstrual pads be free? Menstruation is not a "not a big deal" but an exceptional biological feature gifted to women, not merely a 'woman's or girl's problem'. Nor it is like fairness creams where we have a choice. There is every reason for the government to step in. All aspects associated to health: people, environment, human rights, sustainable development, and others should come under the government's tutelage, to be groomed equally without compromising one in the name of aiding the other. At the same time, the government should also discourage rampant and unnecessary distribution of bad quality pads by anyone and everyone in the name of social service, often short-lived and publicity-oriented, which adds more burden to the environment. We're not living in the '70s; this is an era of social media and cutting-edge technology where positivity spreads like lava on a field while negativity, like wild fire in forest. If each one of us strives for 'dignified menstruation, everyone's confrontation,' then like rice grains, pulses, shaving machine, aftershave lotion, and other items, menstrual pads will also get enlisted in the family's monthly grocery list. Maybe then girls and women can live at peace without the need to wait for everyone to leave at the store to ask the keeper for something that ensures the safe birth of human beings. It's nowhere but in the head. Menstruation-related issues in societies are mostly psychological complications that only go away with mental vaccination.

***

I do not exactly remember when was the last I used a pad but it should be around the time when I was an anesthetic assistant nurse back in Bharatpur Hospital. All my colleague nurses were elder to me. I was the youngest both in looks and experience. I think it was my way with work that I had a cordial relationship with everyone.

I saw them frequently wearing pads and thought maybe they just wore it to work. There would often be large-sized gauge pads and sometimes commercially available ones. In those days, we took pads from the to-be-mother pregnant women admitted to the hospital to stock for poor patients who couldn't afford them. What caught my attention was a sister (as everyone would call a nurse) who took more than necessary. "We work day and night here. If we keep a piece or two for ourselves, we won't suddenly turn into sinners. Here, take this!" she said.

I was hesitant at first but later on they started keeping my share every time they kept for themselves. I took it lest I should be an outcast. It was as easy as wearing an underwear. Good news-you didn't have to wash them. More good news-they could easily be disposed in the hospital.

But there was a constant feeling of repentance in my heart. I knew I was the part of corruption. But I was taking those pads only when everyone took them. Because I couldn't say no as they already used to call me hot pepper for some reason and couldn't say yes either, with content, it put me on the fence of morality.

There were some important tasks we had to do as a team. So, there was no point revolting against them. I was working as an anesthetic assistant. My job was to assist the anesthesiologist to deliver anesthesia and monitor patients during the surgery. But when the anesthetic doctor was on leave, during festivals, or when he was sick, I was the one to do their job. I was doing everything they did.

If you do good job, everyone's happy. But if you make a mistake once, you have to deal with their frowning faces. They could sue me for murder. So, I needed a certificate from the hospital administration to validate my training, which was a tedious task in itself. That's because I was the first of the kind and I was a woman. This was the pad-politics I was fighting against.

When the operation theatre was not at work, we'd gather and do some stuff that helped people. Making pads out of local materials was one of such tasks. The in-charge of our department had a small company that made pads and we helped in every way possible by weaving them into a safe but not-so-elegant-looking handmade pad ever made. Here I learnt why pads do not stick, how they can be made cheaper, and how a margin of profit can be made. The latter was achieved by stuffing coarse and balled-up cotton.

I had a first encounter with such pads when I joined Pokhara Nursing Campus. During the first year, I did not have the faintest idea of what it was. However, in the second year, when I was studying midwifery, I stumbled upon one. The pads those days had a belt on them, at least most of them, but some without it contained two loose bandage strings that could be tied to the belt. This enabled the user to wear the pad and belt like an underwear. Some pads without belts had to be worn by tying it with bandage strings around the waist. Women would feel awkward to wear these because wearing a pad with strings at home was not so popular.

Women too were not aware of what posture they should sleep in and how to manage their clothing. I tried to brief a few women about wearing this type of pad but they ended up leaking blood onto their petticoat, loincloth, sari, and bedsheets. Some women felt comfortable without pads. For them, a cloth wound multiple times around or a piece would do the job. Others wore loins like males to prevent the leakage. I tried to get my head around all these clothing repertoires in the first year of my class and learned a lot.

The third time I had menstruation was during my Nursing Campus years. One could not wear anything but dhoti-like attire, an only option. Either pink or white sari made of cotton. When I wore it, it looked like somebody had put it in my body. I never knew how to wear it; somehow, I made it through the years without its proper knowledge. And without knowing that, you could not perfect the art of substituting a pad.

I had seen my sisters hide blood-stained clothes among other clothes or even at the corner of the wooden pillars of the cow shed. The cloth was roughly one meter. Mine was, too. We didn't throw way the old and overused clothes. They were turned into menstrual cloths. When you don't have enough anything, leave alone new clothes, finding a rugged piece of good-for-nothing piece is just as challenging as getting new clothes.

The second time I menstruated, I had preserved two pieces of worn-out clothes. I added one more when I was sure to leave home for higher studies. My underwear was like the one worn by males, like shorts, but unlike one my father wore, though similar in design and type. In that sense, I was supposed to wear the long piece of cloth by tying it around the top of my locally made underwear. It was a thing which worked like drawstrings to hold the underwear.

Carrying a ball-sized cloth piece at your lower bottom and winding a sari over it, and then appearing confident, happy, and diligent, multitasking at the same time was something every woman including me had to learn.

So it went. Life was a nice bouquet of flowers called compromises.

My menstrual cycle was not regular. My friends worried a lot about this. Back in home too, I overheard people bitching in my back, busy at guesswork on what could have happened to me. But I didn't lose my sleep over it. If anything troubled me, it was the four days of each cycle. Until now, I still had been practicing menstrual dos and don'ts.

My stay during the first year was in the hostel, a house that was at the corner of the avenue, in a corner room. It was the third room from the toilet. Whenever water was scare in the toilet, we used an alternate tap nearby. Our path through the corridor toward the toilet was when no one was around. With people around, the menstruator's journey to the toilet was accompanied by a friend or two who escorted her in between, like bodyguards you could say. Sometimes we jumped the railing in front of the room and ran for it. We dried the stained pieces of cloth and underwear during the day on the playground or the thickets of elephant grass. If that was not possible, we kept them on the railing in front of the room, hidden under other clothes.

During the first few years of menstruation, the catch was to find an appropriate place to hide the pieces of blood-stained cloths, the basics of where and how to dry them. The most challenging of the tasks was the most trivial-sounding: sitting. Sometimes, it was difficult to determine which butt cheek to land first while sitting; I would end up being a tilting airplane. On top of that, the landing totally failed at times due to the leakage of blood from the sides. There's a damp feeling down there, did I make a mess?

And while we stood, each of the friends would look back on the seat as if we dropped coins there. It was to make sure whether we left an indelible imprint on it; however, most of the times the reddened mark would be erasable. The first question that came to my mind was what others would say to this. What if it stains right at the center of two butt cheeks on the outside? It would pretty much be shameful in front of visitors and doctors in the hospital.

These quandaries were quantum theory to me. And the fundamental questions of the universe were 'how do I go to the toilet with the stains?', 'what if there's no water?', 'what if others know about it and laugh?', 'should I drink less water to avoid standing and going to the toilet?', and 'what posture do I sleep in?' This kept me up at night.

The Menstruation Fiasco

Whatever happened, I don't think they knew my menstruation story to any extent. I didn't talk much about it and most of it was to hide it from myself, as much as I could. I remember, at times, a clean piece of cloth assuming a handkerchief did get washed and dried along with other clothes. It was an entirely hush story which I'd only visit when someone talked me into it.

The year following, we moved to a different location. My room was on the first floor past the staircase. Everything we did on the first floor was immediate news to the people living there. Sometimes, daily chores would be public statements. We had with us senior sisters who had passed the A.N.M exams and had a working job, looked more confident than us. They had different way with things than us, even their panties, which used to be tiny red ones, ready-manufactured. I could see their panties, prepared from new cotton threads dried in the sun alongside the aisle. They were at display out in the open unlike mine. I felt awkward in washing and drying my panties. I hid it among other clothes in sections under the staircase.

I'd like to buy clothes like these someday and dry them out in the open for everyone to see. For a person who doesn't get a penny more than 500 rupees every month, buying those clothes was out of the question.

Only did I know that money often came out of a debtor's pocket rather than directly from my father's. Neither my father nor I could dream of extravagant spending on exorbitantly priced items. The expenditure plan was pretty simple. About 350 rupees went to the students' mess. The remaining was just enough to buy my stationeries.

I started saving money. After four months' worth of saved pennies, I bought two brand new nylon undergarments and a meter of a green cotton cloth. One meter split into four pieces would suffice for fourteen good months. I flaunted my washed undergarments out in the open like the seniors did. A sudden surge of menstrual pride and empowerment ran in my body which allowed me to accept it with ease. Much ease.

I practiced wearing those clothes by trial and error. Sometimes, they worked. At other times, they utterly failed. Like every problem had a solution, I fixed them one by one because it was my problem and I knew better than anyone to fix them. My coping mechanism kicked in every time I had to change my ways of managing those clothes on my body.

I had my second menstruation six months after the first. While I was not home the first time it happened, this time it was different. I chose not to tell anyone and tried to cope with it. I couldn't tell this to my sister, too. After all, I had left home without even letting her know. But more than that, the point was I didn't want to be faithful toward elders on menstruation the same way my sisters were.

I managed some pieces of clothes and went to school without the sisters knowing about it. They had hidden the entire process from me, from everybody. But I knew them. I had by then pretty much every idea of who had already menstruated in my school. There were friends whose coping mechanisms, the absorbents, were not working and there were friends who would stay home for a week to avoid such exhibitions. Teachers and students alike would tease them for their monthly visit to maternal home, as they'd feign each time. It was a euphemism for absentees due to menstruation. Later on, they started signaling me about those events.

"Radha, do you see a swelling spot in my lower back?" they'd ask.

"Yes, it's big" or "no, not a bit, just a bit."

When we gathered in the field or toilet during a short break, they turned around their friends like merry-go-round. Clockwise and anti-clockwise with careful eyes of their friends inspecting the merest dots of blunder. "Do you see anything in my skirt?"

"I see it."

"No, you're good."

When they rode bicycles, the questions were frequent and the turnarounds were several times as if they grew a tail. If anyone asked the greatest number of questions, it was none other than Shanta. When we headed back to home from school, she lifted her back off the cycle's seat while on the ride and asked the same question over and over. Every time we drove to soared speeds and waited for each other, I felt she had leaked on her clothes and before I'd offer a look, she'd said, "Is it still good?" We'd guffaw at this. Shanta offered her cycle's rear rack for me and dropped me home.

“You’ve got a patch…Are you serious?” This was how we bid farewell to each other.

These questions were normal and every other girl asked their friends at least once. Each girl had a closed circle of two to five friends who gave honest answers without judgment or mockery.

Nobody ever asked me if I had menstruated. I too at times did not realize I had. But most of the times, I knew because it came big. I don’t know why but I did not tell anyone about this. Not even to Shanta who was my closest friend. Despite she relied on me each moment for feedback, I don’t remember asking her the question even once. When I assured or warned her of her back, I never tried to know more than what was asked of me. While my friends were not looking at me, I’d feel for my bump in the lower back and maintain its position-left, right, slightly forward, backward-and made sure it remained there, worked fine without a hitch.

When I changed my place in the class, I was wary of whether my friends saw it and are already laughing. What if they ask? The merest thought of this made me drip in sweat. What do I do if the cloth bump is to suddenly fall off while walking? I was walking along caught up with all these thoughts when Shanta called me.

“Radha, would you accompany me to the latrine?”

I couldn’t say no. I knew it was important. My bladder was empty because I hadn’t cared to drink water.

Shanta, like always, asked me to go first. I complied. A large pit surrounded by wooden planks on almost all sides-it was one-of-a-kind latrine. In between the planks, there were gaps through which light could pass. But I never cared to notice those gaps. Shanta along with others stood outside looking toward me through that gap. I was certain they're looking toward me. They might be watching for my tiny cloth football that I'd inserted inside my underwear. The merest act of urination was like launching rockets. And this time, it failed.

I lost the rocket. In exasperation, I let loose of the cloth ball which landed into the filth at the center of the pit. It killed the serendipity of the flies around the feces which by now had gathered around the floating ball of cloth.

Even though I walked out of the toilet with a pale face, Shanta didn't ask me anything maybe because her bladder was swelling. I was dying of thirst but couldn't drink water. It made me pee. And pee made me come to the latrine through the long trail and I hated to walk during my menstrual days.

Shanta wanted to drink water and was desperate to join the others at the hand pump but I can tell not as much desperate as I not wanting to go. My mouth was sticky-dry and the sight of water gushing out of the hand pump made me join them too.

I lowered my mouth onto the hand pump's nozzle. Like the water current pushing soft stones at the edge of a river, the flood of water came out of it and pushed against my lips. They remained there as if to test the current and not to sip a bit.

My friends who came out for a break kept on asking why I had a long face. I couldn't show them my demons:

how would I sit with only the underwear in the class? Why didn't I drink water even I was thirsty? The fear of the unknown crippled my senses.

I was the shortest of the five girls amongst several dozen boys in my class. I crawled on my bench and wished never to have to stand again. When I turned back to see my friends' reaction, I couldn't look into the eyes of the boys most of who were like my elder brothers, uncles, and goons of the street. I couldn't look into the eyes of even the ones who were shorter and younger to me.

Everything the teacher said, made no sense throughout. I remembered the cloth ball I let loose in the toilet and that was all I remember. My senses were busy in maintaining the delicate balance of my butt cheeks where I slid my hands under each side, turn by turn like cantilevers to stand the weights. This was the tactic I used to prevent seepage of the blood through the underwear and onto the bench and not to leave a stubborn stain. Ineffaceable. Not just on the bench but also on my confidence.

I was introduced to cloth padding when I saw my sisters do it. Back then, there wouldn't be much clothes to squander for such a thing. My sisters fought over a small piece, snatched, and almost tore it, and I watched them in awe. I didn't understand how people could fight over such a good-for-nothing piece of cloth only to understand later that they were often used by mother for padding the mattresses and by sisters for hiding blood.

In the early days, I stayed away from cloth pieces. Changing clothes, bathing, and washing were my escape route. After fighting all the difficult wars, my menstruation-related anxiety was limited to only the first day. Afterwards, I felt royal: all rest and no play made me a slothful princess.

In fact, one can use any type of padding material that soaks blood depending on what you can afford. Before using, however, one needs to know its pros and cons. As far as I'm concerned, the best that suits me is a clean cotton cloth or a piece of cotton blanket cover, though it is often impractical to wash it repeatedly especially if you travel. In that case, I usually take to tampons and sometimes the non-decomposable commercial pad. I haven't gathered enough commitment in all these eyes for a cup. I realized I waited long for decomposable pads.

November, 2018 onwards, Radha Paudel Foundation has started the production of decomposable menstrual pads in coordination with Active Women's Platform for Justice in Chitwan. Fiber-made decomposable, reusable pads were produced since 2014 under my leadership, through rigorous training among men and women of Jumla and Kalikot districts. In the course of training on Dignified Menstruation, the members of the foundation including I had imparted pad-making trainings to teachers, students, guardians, and health workers of Sindhupalchowk, Nuwakot, and Chitwan districts. The pads we made had a pouch that could attach on an underwear and to which pieces of clothes could fit. One didn't need exceptional tailoring skills to stitch such a pad; anyone who knew to stitch could do the job. These pads were of different models but all of them were designed to not give women the experience I had in the school latrine. Depending on the quality of the fiber, two to five pads served for an entire year of usage.

Many women use shreds or loin-type cloths suitable for low-income families, families striving for environmental-friendly footprints, and rural areas where commercially available pads are either not accessible or difficult to come by in terms of cost. A cotton pad only lasts for about four hours. To make it reusable, it has to be sun-dried for at least three additional hours in scorching heat to kill the germs. If it's raining or snowing, then it can also be dried with the heat of the hearth's fire. Or if available, ironing would do the job. Poorly maintained pads can easily give an infection. Sometimes, they even turn into brooding homes for maggots.

Commercially available pads should be changed at the interval of at least five hours. After use, they should be disposed in a safe place. It's best not to burn it. Instead, they can be buried which is relatively feasible option. One has to encase the waste in a paper or plastic before burying so that dogs don't waste their time carrying them from place to place, or the wind blowing them. That way, neither flies are encouraged nor are the passers-by discouraged.

However, commercial pads do not decompose for 200 to 1000 years. They are frequent pollutants and the exposure to their chemicals is hazardous in many ways which might lead to allergic reactions, infection, and even-as many claim-cancer due to absorptive agents.

When I look back, I remember my mother using none of these safety items but improvising by thickening the folds of the sari or loincloth in the vaginal region. She sat with care when on menstruation. Today, it is more or less the same. She's no more. But if she had been alive, she'd be in her menopausal days.

The same trend has continued even today wherever I go-be it Kapilvastu, Ramechhap, Baitadi, or Mugu. Majority of women do not wear an underwear or petticoat. Girls in particular wear multiple trousers or traditional wrap-around towels and avoid public places. They bathe and wash in a rivulet far off. Women, like my mother, fold the cloth they're wearing multiple times and shove it in their vaginal front. If they sense bleeding, they squat as if to urinate to clean off the blood and further wind the clothes they've worn. More windings each time the gush of blood wet their cloth.

Girls and women do this out of compulsion and ignorance, to talk superficially, and pragmatically due to economic hardships. There are places in the country where women wash the same clothes multiple times a day but there are also places where the same cloth is worn for multiple days, four or five. Nevertheless, not all rural or economically backward women do this. Some women take sanitation so seriously, they end up meeting the budget for underwear and cotton clothes by any means. But they are rare. When people start treating menstruation not just as a sanitation but also a social issue, solutions will come up one after the other, starting from intention.

Blood-Soaked Men

Lainchaur, Chamunda Bindrasaini, Dailekh

The air was boiling hot. I somehow managed to walk on the semi-glistening road to the destination.

Two young women, Lalshara Biswakarma, 14, and Tulasha Shahi, 19, had died from snake bike in a Chhaupadi shed because neither were rushed to a hospital on time. Nobody came to their rescue. Agonized by the news, I managed to visit the place twice as a social worker, with the district co-ordination committee members.

Dailekh district had gone to the then Nepal Communist Party (United Marxist-Leninist; CPN-UML) during the election. When they knew I had come to talk on menstruation, the party cadres of CPN-UML, Nepali Congress, and the Nepal Communist Party (Maoist) took to verbal dissuasion. This was the first case of an FIR filed in the history of the country.

"You let our district down. Who files a complaint on the behalf of a dead person? Such an uncivilized person you are!" I was greeted benevolently-like that-as soon as I reached. "Fill the village with Christians because observing menstrual 'rites' is a Hindu tradition."

One of them suggested that I read Upanishads and get religiously 'woke', get educated on tradition. I slid my hand into the bag and pulled out the tiny book along with several blue and red pamphlets.

“Read this,” I said handing the book of constitution to them. “And here…these are your manifesto declarations.” I read the lines from their party manifestoes.

They didn’t say a word but it didn’t end there. By whatever way, I turned up in their good books and was invited as a speaker later on in a program the party men organized.

Not just Dailekh, I’ve taken enough verbal shots from Baitadi, Jumla, Kalikot, Chitwan, Parsa, Mahottari, and other districts from people of all professions: journalists, human rights activists, teachers, among others. I remember one of the incidents when a teacher for thirty-seven years, worked in semi-urban area, the then principal of a school, threatened me to shower with Chandannath Baba’s rice grains. (Chandannath Baba was a man from Kashmir and is believed to have come to Jumla during the Kallala dynasty in Jumla and brought the statue of Dattatreya monk along. In his honour, people constructed a temple at the spot. The rice grains offered to him and sprinkled on anyone is believed to cause harm as intended.)

Whether the teacher wanted to turn me crazy or dead, I’m not sure. But he was no more a teacher to me. What more to expect from a person like him who teaches menstrual blood is impure? How many brains has he washed until now-Shova Shakya from Lalitpur, my accompanying acquaintance, had written a column on Nagarik Daily newspaper on this verbal scowl.

To talk of witch doctors and religious fanatics alike is the same story told with different flavor; it doesn’t matter where they are from or which community they belong, the oppose the idea of dignified menstruation. These are the people who benefit from the nourishment of superstition. It doesn't matter whether they themselves subscribe to such fallacious beliefs but as long as people consult them for something as natural as menstruation, they keep earning from the change of seasons. They earn their living propagating lies and that's why people like us who speak the truth become the victims of their verbal insults and curses. Few men even got drunk and shouted out loud in front of our temporary residence in those places. Sometimes, the verbal insults escalated into physical confrontation. But whenever those hands which were raised to harm us rested on their chests for the pursuit of truth, so far, the ones who tried, ultimately ended up with self-criticism.

I would never be deterred to fight the war of bringing people to truths who oppose the truths for 'theirs'. If treated with compassion, dacoits can turn into monks, why not mortal men? Most of the times, they would shake hands and walk on our footsteps to fight against menstruation-related practices. And I would gleam from inside. One at a time, I would say.

Seeking a Man

Irked by people's abuse and censure, I was seeking a man who, like me, would stand with a conscience against menstrual malpractices. A man who'd be ready to be an armor for women's rights, and whom I could call a good man-or as the world says, a 'real man.' I was in search of a man whom I could bow.

I looked for the man in women's groups and among shamans and politicians. They all disappointed me. I didn't succumb to defeat.

Then this happened:

I was walking past the municipality office toward the school, descending down a crest and traversing another hillock's line of settlements when I encountered a wooden house laid with mud and brick. There on the ground floor, I saw a man, who during the morning rain was boiling milk. His name was Ishwor Bohora.

Ishwor seemed complaining.

"When I returned home in the evening, my wife said: 'our daughter had menstruated and she's about to leave for the jungle.' I had an argument with my wife against sending her to the jungle," Bohara said. "I pulled my daughter by her arm, brought her home, and kept her inside. She slept on one bed; we slept on the other. It's not a big deal, you see-menstruation is only a natural process." Happiness shimmered in Ishwor's eyes.

“It wasn’t easy at all. At least it wasn’t meant to be. We live with our mother. Father’s dead. She didn’t eat with us for three months. Even the neighbors boycotted. We didn’t stop to speak out, to sort things out. Slowly, mother joined us and later the neighbors.”

***

It was five in the morning in Jumla, toward the end of Ashoj. Our home was five minutes’ walk from Khalanga bazaar, opposite the Tila river. I was awake, but my eyes were closed. I didn’t feel like opening them because there was nothing to do on waking up. There was no internet to reach the world from the bed and no morning fire to heat the body. The landlords were asleep. Together with friends from Germany and Austria, we waited for the interaction program to start at seven.

Kalika, her son, and his friend-we all slept in a single room. I’ve named this room Miteri Homestay. I’ve built a knack for staying in people’s homes from village to village, give some money or gifts to the hosts, and bid them goodbye in the morning.

They gave me a bed to sleep out of courtesy, while others slept on the floor. My friends were next door.

Bajyai! Bajyai!

“Open the door…Make a haste. It’s freezing outside.”

Bajyai (opening the door): “What is it? Why’re you so restless in this early cold morning?”

"I'm alone and I'm scared," the granddaughter said.

"Where're your parents?" bajyai asked.

"My mother turned untouchable. She went to the cow shed taking my brother. Father's gone to the bazaar." The poor girl nearly burst into tears. "I feel scared." She spoke in a small voice again.

Her mother was a health worker, a permanent employee of the Nepal Government. Her father, and his sister and brother-everyone is employed in their own ways. Even her grandfather was a famous politician and social worker during his time. Her house was in the heart of Khalanga bazaar. Her husband-young and agile-was an employee of an NGO for women's empowerment. They had access to the internet, both in her husband's and mother's.

Troubled by such thoughts, I couldn't fall asleep. It was an inexplicably hollow feeling. Disheartened, I came downstairs. No one had awakened. I looked for the child's mother whom I had met on the way yesterday evening. I was wondering where she had been all this time. Perhaps the cowshed? Or maybe her maternal home's cowshed-or made arrangements at her aunt's?

When I walked out of the latrine, I heard a child's voice and called her: "Hey sister, over here."

"Yes, fupu?" she spoke to me in a thin voice.

I returned to the door and walked in.

She clutched her three-month-old son on her lap and sat on a filthy and tattered bedsheet, and a similar blanket, with a torn cover and balls of cotton condensed at places that lay beside her. The floor was filthy too: in one corner lay the household tidbits-a bundle of firewood, ropes, and a pair of old shoes along with a heap of other items.

I turned on the cellphone's flashlight, looked around, and asked, "What do you think you're doing?" You still don't know how it happens? Didn't you tell me yesterday that you gave a training against observing menstrual rites? And yet you have been observing the same thing? How can you convince others not to? Isn't this a sin?

She was silent and stared at the floor. The son wailed-and I knew he didn't cry of hunger but of cold or perhaps of disgust. Maybe the fur was too coarse for him. Look at this child's life! He doesn't bleed every month, but because of you he too has to observe the rites. His menstrual rites begin right after three months of his birth.

If the child is older and sleeping with the mother during her menstrual cycle, s/he is bathed, sprinkled with sunpaani (literally: gold water, holy water that cleanses the body), and dressed in fresh clothes. Only when he's become pure, the other members of the family touch him. This tradition is prevalent in many areas of the country and is both unnecessary torture and a practice yoked upon the child.

In the cities, a child sleeps with their mother till five or seven. Yet, in Western Nepal, the son sleeps with his mother until he leaves home for education or work. Thus, men also observe menstrual rites for lifetime. Her husband leaving the house early in the morning is also a way of observing this rite.

If the child is matured enough and wears a janai (a sacred thread worn by male boys and rarely girls, after Upanayana ritual, which religiously fixes the boy a guru and makes him eligible for performing death rites) and if he mistakenly touches menstruating mother, sisters, sister-in-law, daughter-in-law, wife, or any other woman, he has to take the trouble of either bathing or replacing his janai. If not, sprinkling gold-water or cow-urine is a common practice of purification.

Bathing or getting cleaned is not innately wrong per se. But all the activities performed in the name of purification just because a man touched a menstruating woman are the byproducts of erroneous thinking. They are useless practices which have been hampering men, too. Men have been mobilized to uphold such superstitions. People who advocate for observing such rites, who think it's better to follow the tradition, often question: Why all this fuss about bathing?

Fine, a menstruating woman avoids touching a man. Maybe she has to ponder another path or way, adding more trouble. With other don't-do-this-and-that, there's a lot of anxiety for women. However, the society has put an added stress on men as well. To evade a menstruating woman and be far from her, a man has to plot alternative ways unnecessarily, seek mediators, and follow prerequisites which have been taxing them for time immemorial.

It's widely observed in the society that when a woman menstruates, the house chores she'd be doing such as cooking, looking after the children, and daily worship among others, in absence of other women, are done by men. It's good for men that they do such activities at least once in a while.

But it would be the best if they do it all the time.

A house is a common place for both men and women, and hence the chores should be done by both of them, irrespective. It becomes more necessary for men to indulge themselves in house chores in houses where both men and women work outside. Whether women work outside or not, they need rest. They are always in need of love, help, and support from their husbands and families. The idea that a man's wife menstruated and so he should do household work is absolutely discriminatory to women. It reinforces that woman are made for household chores and it's the duty of men to help them only when they are physically unfit. This not just puts women in jeopardy towards familial exploitation more but also adds physical and mental burden to men who never perform such arduous tasks. Those men who undertake stressful jobs outside find a difficult time maintaining both if they do it occasionally.

***

Among men I wished to seek for my mission, one of them would be my father. We had gone to Dailekh district in 2017 B.S. while we were traveling to Jumla. When he shared about gods and tradition and how they were unrelated to the malpractice, I was speechless. I knew he'd revolt but this way, it wasn't expected. I kept staring at his face. A mixture of pride and happiness surged inside. It was a startling moment to see him advocate for menstruation rights. I hadn't even hinted him anything about the topic. How did my father who didn't see school classrooms come up with such words of wisdom out of the blue?

I was looking at the community's faces; the community was looking at my father's. Needless to say, men play a significant role in making the lives of daughters better during menstruation. I have to seek many men like my father-those without formal education but with a greater rational faculty.

It’s Okay to Be Weak

Owing to them becoming weak, many women assume that they should observe the menstrual rites. Others say they don’t have the obligation to be together with their demanding husbands whenever he wants. In reality, both arguments are illogical.

In some places, when a girl menstruates for the first time, she’s allowed to meet her friends. But such interaction isn’t encouraged afterward. Those girls who’re happy because of isolation or want to experience menstruation, don’t share the same experience later on. It is not as easy as it sounds.

Because some women feel they get time to stay with their friends without fretting over the household work and also can do outside chores, they feel happy every month, but not for long. These are all byproducts of laden-with responsibilities and discriminations. In a similar manner, some women in their late postpartum days also feel the same-try and feel rejuvenated for getting rest. These women have to go back to their usual tasks and nothing will change for them. Child-bearing is in fact a once-or-twice-in-a-lifetime recess (in some cases more but without luck) for women.

***

Child-bearing and menstruation are innately natural phenomena. In a group of 100 pregnant women (anyone from anywhere), eighty-five bear a child themselves while in ten of them, the labor pain has to be induced and they might need forceps/machines to deliver the baby. The remaining five need a caesarian section.

If a new born child receives adequate food and clothes, devoid of social, cultural, and gender discrimination; contrary to the common Nepali belief, the mother doesn't have to rest for an extended period. We have seen numerous examples of mothers going home from hospitals few hours after delivery and taking care of themselves and the child. The readiness and preparedness with which the delivery of a newborn is carried out depend on the mental and physical well-being of the mother.

Likewise, during the time of menstruation, around eighty-five out of 100 women know they're about to bleed. Even then, symptoms vary from person to person depending on the hormonal changes in woman's body. Headaches, nausea, vomiting, loss of appetite, irritation, anger, backache, stomachache, and calf pain are common symptoms.

Studies have shown that only five out of 100 people show serious symptoms like excessive vomiting, unconsciousness, acute stomach pain, and prolonged backache. In such cases, they need special attention and medical care. Keeping these things in mind, some western companies have started offering paid days leave to women during menstruation.

When only normal symptoms are seen, considering them weak is equally wrong. Doing light work, interacting with friends, reading a book, listening to music, working together with family members, and talking to other women gives women emotional comfort. Likewise, wrapping a long cloth or belt around the waist and drinking a lot of fluids comfort them to an even greater extent. When women do these activities, menstruation may not seem so problematic.

Girls, on the other hand, regularly miss schools because of cramps which they, in few cases, make a big deal. When it comes to studies and career, they have to learn to treat menstruation like peeing or having a painful jerk after a fall, of course with pain of different intensities, and that too every month. Except girls who have excruciating cramps and agonizing hormonal imbalances, the rest should attend their schools and other creative activities because it might then be habitual to skip school or work and fall in the habit of giving it up just because of an ongoing bodily function. Some girls take to menstruation as an escape to skipping classes because they're not good in studies, probably have a bad school environment, or are suffering from emotional and psychological problems. Parents should monitor their children's regularity to school and health during menstrual cycles. That way, they can prevent their daughters to evade school assignments, project works, and exams.

However, some girls fear ostracism at school because of usual handling problems of menstrual blood. The teachers and fellow students see blood 'leakage' as a wardrobe malfunction-or rather bodily malfunction, and sometimes mock them. Most schools do not have female-friendly toilets and bathrooms. Disposing used products is another such problem. When in class, girls feel shy to ask their teachers to let them out because they had a leakage. Teachers seem not to understand this at best, and at worst, exhibit unfriendly and indifferent disciplinary regulation: not letting students go out more than once. Shallow, indeed. Because of all these reasons, girls skip classes more often than boys and remain behind in course activities. What's more unfortunate is-some of them skip or limit their studies up to school level never to join college, while others never return back to school for good.

Sex is Not Man's Innate Right

First-those husbands who're indifferent to their wives' plight and the lascivious ones often seek the body of their wives during menstruation, at any cost. Second-a woman is supposed to get ready whenever her men desires.

Both are absolutely wrong.

That sex is a man's innate right is an epitome of faulty patriarchal thinking. This is another instance of violence against women. To consider that a woman has to take it as her duty to unwillingly fulfill her husband's desire is misguided though it might sound perfectly natural to many. To be unable to negotiate with her husband or partner against it is to be ignorant and to accept violence. To consider oneself guilty and be ready for a man's untamed and untimed desires are examples of patriarchal traps. A woman doesn't have to be ready for a man's pleasure over one's pain, misery, and unhappiness as much as a man. There's no need to feel shame, fear, or guilt. And there's no need to be a slave to such demeanor.

If a wife or a mother menstruates during shraddha (a Hindu ceremony in which you mold pudding into a sphere, called pinda, and offer it to the dead ancestors to pay them homage) or any other religious ceremony, the work either gets stopped or postponed. If any such event is to occur, all members of the family are saddened and feel at loss, especially men who work at the office. One way or another, men too have been observing lifelong menstrual rites.

Almost all men-teachers, health workers, government employees, development workers, human rights activists, pundits, shamans-are the same when it comes to menstrual rights. They voice for women's rights for the sake of their jobs, posts, prestige, or projects. They seem to express commitment in the acts too.

"Women are obstinate and keep observing menstrual rites despite our constant discouragement," they say. "They want to save the age-old tradition. Even though they're liberal at work, they want to follow the customs when at home." One gets to hear such cacophonic clarifications often, guised in men's voices.

Many men do not know what menstruation even means. Though they cherish vague bookish knowledge, they don't exactly understand what they're talking about. Men who admit what they've been doing till now is wrong are hard to find. Men are being misguided by their home, society, school, media, politics, and religion. They've been hearing about impurity, filth, congealed blood, and which they have internalized as nothing but reality. They have been harboring irrational fears such as what if I, my family, or cattle fall sick?

Despite the diverse socio-economic conditions, men as compared to women, often go out of their houses, interact with society, and have easy access to mass communication, in the context of Nepal. So, they are naturally aware of both positive and negative aspects of menstruation. If they're really against women observing the menstrual rites, why don't they discuss this with their families? Like Ishwor Bohora, why don't they bring back their daughters and wives by their arms who leave home when they menstruate?

Why don't they give them food and shelter in their houses? Why do they hesitate to help their mothers, sisters, wives, and daughters? Why do they feel ashamed or afraid to talk openly about menstruation?

Their refusal to openly discuss menstruation has been indirectly establishing it as a taboo. Why can't they admit that customs are social constructs? Biology is fixed but tradition is fluid. It is dynamic, always in flux. Why can't men say they should scientifically adapt the customs and tradition as per the time and age? There are so many topics where men's knowledge has fallen behind.

For the record, on April 14, 2018, when the Prime Minister addressed the nation from the Rara Lake, he neither confirmed staying in a cowshed during menstruation is against the law nor did he guarantee female-friendly education when discussing school admission campaigns. This is just a stand-in for historically biased thinking and actions against women. This impoverished thinking, which carries significant meaning, results from the unacknowledged fact that prosperity is when men with higher authorities do better things, without women's meaningful participation.

Many men don't need position and power to speak against injustice. They have brought the women observing the menstrual rites from the cowshed to the house and have taken leadership for women's human rights. All it takes is determination and courage, not money and power. This, however, forms a small minority which are shadowed by other dominant voices.

I started the revolution against observing menstrual rites from my home. My 81-year-old widowed father, who has never seen the interior of a school, still practices the

Hindu culture and performs puja and Shraddha. He never asked his daughters, daughters-in-law, or granddaughters out of barring concern if they are menstruating. He doesn't forbid them from celebrating festivals and going to temples.

Once in Dalikeh, I was discussing menstruation from a chaur, an open field. There was something some people said which I still remember: "Females shouldn't consume milk, yogurt, meat-fish, and fruits during menstruation. If they touch, cows-buffaloes fall sick and their milk dry out. Those quadrupeds may as well die-or worse, may start climbing trees! Those women shouldn't go to homes, temples, religious ceremonies, or marriages. They shouldn't ever touch janai-wearing men or the shamans because that risks their good health. The gods and the ancestors will get angry."

I urged them to speak out their fears and anxiety and listened to what they had to say.

At a distance, in the right corner, squatting as if about to defecate, was a man who was idly playing with a stone with his right hand. He sprung up suddenly and said:

"Look, I have planted this stone right here, upright. If someone plucks flowers and places them over it, everybody will start worshipping it as a god. And in the afternoon, they will festoon the entire field with vermillion, flowers, and prayer flags. Maybe in another five to six months, some generous villagers will come together to build a temple. When I was a child, there wasn't any hospital. People barely recovered from illnesses. Now, there are hospitals everywhere, almost on every doorstep. Radios and mobile phones are in every houses. Even if we keep chanting the names of the gods, many daughters will die. Our laps will still be empty. Can we rely on religious offerings to make our life better? I am a Hindu, but ever since this daughter has returned with a nursing degree, I haven't asked her to observe menstrual rites. We have known and understood, and our granddaughters have received happiness . . ."

We rarely get to hear such words of wisdom from a group of people a majority of whom believe in superstition.

In another such event, the granddaughter in a religious family who was observing a week-long religious ceremony menstruated. The school was running. She, who was still going to school, bought a menstrual pad from the market. During the day time, she went to her school. In the mornings and evenings, she played around the house and helped in the kitchen. Only on the third day, she disclosed this to her mother. For her, there was no point in hiding or observing the rites. But later she started to hide. She sneaked into her mother's room and stole her pads. Or she'd use the money given to her for snacks. The mother started worrying, wondering if her daughter's cycles were irregular or bad.

The mother remembered the conversations of women back in the days during the fieldwork in her maternal village that irregular menstruation was the work of an unhealthy uterus and an anemic body. They also said that nobody would marry such girls, and even if they did, she won't have babies. Having no babies meant a wrecked family. Out of this anxiety, the mother went to a private medical facility and bought "energy-giving" iron syrup for her daughter. Yet, the daughter didn't take the medicine regularly. When the mother cajoled her, she'd take the syrup; otherwise, she didn't bother.

Another granddaughter got more scared during her time. She stayed in her friend's house for five days, afraid as she was of her grandmother. She didn't quit school but later when she realized it was not a big deal, her confidence boosted. She persuaded her grandmother to allow tika (reddened paste of paddy grains, curd, and abir-the mixture of colors and mica) during Dashain and Tihar, even when she had her meastruation.

The third granddaughter didn't even realize she menstruated. Luckily, it was a holiday and everyone was home. Her aunts saw and taught her to wear underwear and fix menstrual pads onto them. They talked with her father and made father and daughter go to buy stuff. The duo took a tour of the market. The little girl bought some underwear and the father bought snacks for her. They returned home only in the evening.

Whenever they turned out to be nine or ten, I'd stay with my nieces during the holidays for a chat. We talked about menstruation. I often advised their parents-that it's difficult for girls to live a mannered life in a society entangled with superstition and orthodoxy. If you hear the same thing over and over from your family of few, and then the society of dozens, it feels whatever they've been doing-spreading illusions that are-is almost true. But if one discusses such topics continuously, shattering no myths is impossible.

A Psychological Fear

Kathmandu Airport.

The sun was about to set. I reprimanded Priya and Julia sardonically throughout the journey, but was overwhelmed with emotions when I saw them off in a taxi. "Radha didi! Don't forget to tell the story of tampons," they shouted from a taxi window which they had lowered. "Ha-ha."

As the taxi sped up, their laughter dimmed and trailed away. Yet, what remained with me was their mirth, their conversation-luminous like the full moon. The farther they went, the shinier it became.

***

Srinagar, Humla.

The clock struck 9 p.m.

It all began in the courtyard. Priya and Julia, two volunteers from America, rested on the spread tarpaulin. Squatted on the edge of the wall were Bhim from Kavre and Bishnu from Mugu, listening to the ongoing conversation. Baje (for old man, our porter) came up to me and whispered into my ear. "Madam, I won't be coming tomorrow to carry the bags!"

I was astonished. Who should we find to carry the bags?

"Why? What happened? Are you not feeling well, Baje?"

Baje wasn't a part of the predetermined team. He was a new crewmember arranged after our stay in a place called Bolding in Bajura district for a night. As Julia and Priya figured they couldn't carry the load by themselves, I had to request the landlord to find a porter, and Baje had appeared the next morning when we were about to leave. As we left the house, the landlord shouted from the terrace, "Madam, he is a Brahmin. Be heeded!"

Baje wore a grey daura-suruwal, a black waistcoat, and a thin, cotton cummerbund. "I had an operation in the stomach about three years ago, so I can't carry much load," he had said in the beginning. So, I assumed he'd hurt his waist. That's why the landlord must have advised us. But then it could also be that the landlord said not to touch him when menstruating? After all, we're three women here. Or he must be demanding because he had been carrying the loads of foreigners and wanted more money."

"No, nothing has happened," Baje said.

"What happened? Did you get any news from home? Do you have to return?"

"No, no." He spoke as if he were about to make amends.

"So, what happened? Are the bags too heavy?"

I knew the bags weren't heavy. I had called Baje to make it easy for girls who were unaccustomed to climbing the hills, apart from assisting the team. If something is to happen on the way, who could we find in the month of Asar? The way Baje was mincing his words infuriated me. But I asked in a calm voice: "Tell us, Baje, what's wrong? Why can't you carry the load?"

Baje made excuses, worried that he might have to eat food touched by menstruating women. Yet, he couldn't speak his mind. In a way, the situation was comical.

"What should we do, Baje? Please tell us," I said suppressing my laughter. "Is it because of the cooking? You can cook yourself if that is the case. We can eat whatever you cook, alright?"

Baje's lips curled into a smile, and he nodded in agreement. We had already put some string beans on the stove. Sahuji (owner) was chopping potatoes. I said in a pleading voice, "Bhai, I completely forgot to tell you before. In fact, he's a Brahmin priest and doesn't eat food cooked by others. You might have cooked food for us. Don't you worry, I'll pay for that. Baje will cook the food for us, okay?"

"Please clean the kitchen once and put the utensils there. Give us some rice and potatoes. Baje will cook for us." I said abruptly without waiting for a reply.

I saw him nodding his head in affirmation but didn't wait for his reaction.

Delighted, Baje ran along the whitish trail-from where one could hear Humla Karnali rumbling and raging. The young man from the hotel started cleaning the stove. I ran along with the waves of emotions along with the moving tip of his broomstick.

After meeting Baje in Bolding, we had some snacks at Karishma Hotel in Sakachaur. More than our expectation, the hotel turned out to be clean and managed. Afterward, I conversed with people outside the hotel letting the tap water run across my fingers. I walked in only when I was called.

I was astonished to see Baje gobbling boiled eggs. A while after, he munched on instant noodles. I had ordered vegetarian food for me and him. I couldn't contain my curiosity and said, "Since noodles are chicken-flavored and touched by others, many Brahmins do not eat them, let alone the eggs! How can you, Baje?"

There wasn't any trace of shame, anxiety, regret, or fear in Baje's face. With great confidence and energy, he spoke: "It's okay to eat while traveling madam. If I don't eat like this, I won't be able to walk. One doesn't get to eat eggs daily, so should grab the chance!" I pointed toward the neighbors and joked, "Listen to your pandit's talk! He's the one who's going to perform religious ceremonies tomorrow."

My mind was but wandering toward Sakachaur. The sun had been fiercer by the time we were done eating snacks. On the left was a mountain of rocks and on the right Karnali flowed at its own pace. The girls couldn't walk as they were exhausted and dehydrated. I coupled the team as men and women so they could walk easily. As soon as I paired them up, Julia shouted.

"Radha! Guess what happened to me?"

It turned out to be true. She menstruated. Priya convulsed with laughter and said, "We should send her to the cowshed, Radha didi, the cowshed!" Priya could only say the word didi in Nepali. Since she was habituated in calling didi to her fupu, she could say that to me.

Julia got a little scared. She was also Priya's tennis partner. Since Julia's parents had trusted me with the responsibility, they had sent Julia along to visit us in Nepal.

They knew about Chhaupadi from their parents. I had already taught them how to be quiet and clandestine during menstruation. I asked them to take their tampons out. Finding a toilet on the way was out of the question, though the signboards as soon as we entered Kolti boasted: 'Welcome to Open Defecation & Chhaupadi-Free Zone'.

"Go help Julia use a tampon at the back of the house." I persuaded Priya pointing at the rubble.

Julia had never relieved herself by squatting, and that too in an open space!

I advised her again, "Nothing will happen. Only those who fear a lot and believe in spirits might shiver and fall sick. We are beside the road, with no hospital nearby, no means of transportation. Just keep on walking and say nothing, and hide the blood. I've done this many times, especially when trekking!"

They paired up again and walked together, ahead of us. Bishnu said nothing but yes and no. Baje laughed along. Since we had lost the other water-carrying pot, we depended on one. So, the handed the bottle to Baje first and drank from it later. They gave him a piece of the same chocolate he had been eating to Baje first. And they walked together!

Priya's father was a Nepali. He worked as a successful tennis coach in the US. Her grandfather lived in Nepal and looked the same age as Baje. That might be why Baje had received much love and respect even though he was a nuisance at times. Everyone called him baajyya-just like Priya would call her grandfather.

The rice is almost ready. The fire is the same and so is the water. The uncooked rice, potatoes, and beans are all the same. Only the cook is different: then a young man, now an old man.

Meanwhile, Julia cleaned herself. She changed her underwear and tampon. Then, the two girls ate rice after freshening up. I was the sole audience. Molding these two girls according to convenience and practice was my responsibility.

That hotel wasn't really a hotel. The village was above the new motorway, and the hotel was established to cater to the wayfarers. An open hearth gaped outside, and above it was a floor enclosed on two sides. There was a small general store inside. Another room was attached to that store and the road. Wrappers of noodles, packets of tobacco, and butt-ends of cigarettes, along with the empty bottles of alcohol scattered all over. I asked them to clean the place by separating the wooden boards on one side and the shelf on the other. Men lay on one side, women on the other. We tried but couldn't sleep. There was no latrine, no room door, and not even sleeping beds. Only a room full of sleeping bags!

"Baje, what were those 'Chhaupadi Free Zone' signs in the village?" I asked.

"Ah, nothing!" Baje scoffed. "No, it doesn't suit me, not a bit. Even when I go out to the bazaar, I get terrible headaches because of the risk of touching a menstruating woman. I shiver all over, my ancestors get angry! That is why I enter the home only after bathing and performing a puja." Baje started talking in great excitement.

"Madam, my entire family is the family of priests! I learned priest-work from Benaras. My grandfather, great grandfather-they all learned to do jajaman (conducting religious rites in their Hindu clients' home). My son is also into it these days. He's doing it in Gokarna in Kathmandu."

I convulsed with laughter. You shiver on touching menstruating women? 'Oh, for sure you'd shiver, old man! You've been walking with a menstruating girl all day long, eating with her, taking rest, and helping her climb and descend. You're full of hogwash!' I said to myself.

Girls who have never walked on hills don't know how to trek uphill, downhill, toward the rugged terrains. Whenever such a trail appeared, Baje either clambered up and extended his hand toward the girls or walked by interlocking Julia's hand onto his as if forming a chain. Sometimes, he stood on a low level, let the girls climb first, and reached their extended arm. And now he talked of shivering and the ancestors getting angry!

I yes-ed to Baje's words each time. "Julia is menstruating. That's why she went to the latrine." I could have said this to Baje. What would have happened if I had said it then? I didn't know and I was not prepared to see.

***

Setting out early in the morning would be a wise idea. Once the sun comes up, it becomes difficult to walk. With this plan on my mind, I woke everyone up, and got ready. While I had gone to pay for food and accommodation, I heard Julia's booming voice: "Radha didi, Priya's bleeding!"

I assumed Priya menstruated, too. Two girls in a row. Not today!

Droplets of blood spluttered out of Priya's nostrils. Each time it did, she soaked the blood with a handkerchief. Among owners of the horses and mules making their regular journeys, one of them stopped and reassured: "It's only a nosebleed. Must be the heat. Don't worry, it'll stop in a minute or two."

We started searching for medicinal herbs. Priya went on crying. I asked her to lie flat on the ground, but she'd bend over to cry. Rather than swallowing the blood with the spit, she'd cough forcibly. The bleeding didn't stop. It came out gushing. We were stranded in a difficult place. It would take us two days on foot to reach Gamghadi or Kolti. We raised the cellphones up in the air and displayed it in every other direction. The network was dead.

I put my shawl and tissue paper inside the nostrils, applied some pressure, and tried hard to use the remnants of my wisdom, recollecting my training in nursing. Taking a tampon from Julia's bag, I placed it in Priya's nose. It worked! Men sitting around were surprised. The bleeding had stopped yet not completely. What a magical tampon! Actually, it was because the blood had almost clotted. In any case, the tampon had worked fine.

Our journey didn't stop, neither did Priya's bleeding, properly. When she coughed, her mouth flushed out phlegm covered in blood. If the men walking ahead of us had a nosebleed, they'd halt and insert a tampon inside their nostrils. The girls shared water and chocolates with them, and would tell me about it. The long journey continued. The girls got tired, hungry, thirsty, sunburned all at the same time-dropped their bags to take a rest. But nobody turned insane suddenly. Nobody had a headache. Everyone reached their destination, sharing the laughter.

We reached Bhigau in Mugu district. Baje wrapped the same towel around his waist and cooked food. We heeded to Baje's words and ate our food.

The Formula Worked

She arrived late today.

"I got stuck in traffic," she said. I had received the news from the reception.

"It was easy, isn't it? It must be the traffic of the ants!" I smiled.

She walked up to me restlessly and whispered happily into my ears: "Thank you, didi. Your formula worked."

This was how I conjured up the 'formula':

It was 5:30 in the evening. Everyone had left work. Office-going Kathmanduits are people always in a rush, either in the mornings on their way or when back home in the evenings. However, Salsa was quiet. When I had descended from the third floor to do a quick desk check, I saw the sun's golden rays reflecting off the western mountains. Out on the balcony sat a weather-beaten chair. She spread unhappiness around sitting on that rickety chair and looked as bedraggled as that pale chair.

"Hey, Salsa! What happened? Aren't you feeling well? And don't you have a home to go?" I asked. "Your children might give you a divorce!"

"I have to go. Where can I go except home, didi? But I don't really want to be at home today," Salsa spoke with a heavy heart, as if unbounded pain and suffocation hid inside. Her husband worked outside Kathmandu, and Salsa lived with her children and in-laws.

"It isn't something I wouldn't tell you, didi. My husband came home today. For whatever purpose he came, I am not fit for that."

"Husband's arrival is good news, isn't it?" I mocked.

She got a little irritated and said, "I agree, but he could've called at least. He says he came early to surprise me, that idiot!" Her anger for her husband turned into endearment in no time. "Other times would have been perfect, but today I'm menstruating."

"Where do you sleep when you menstruate?" I asked.

"Same room, but I sleep on the floor."

"Why would you sleep on the floor?"

"I've been sleeping like that ever since we moved to Kathmandu. Back in the village, we had separate rooms. We don't even have enough rooms here. When we have guests, that's more trouble!"

"Look, Salsa," I said, "you know I am a nurse. I'll tell you what I know and leave the rest to you." Like every other day, I spoke openly: "You two love and respect each other. If he doesn't feel disgusted and if you don't feel scared or uncomfortable, there is no problem. The books tell you the same thing: there are fewer chances of conception. The blood will reduce friction and pain. Since you two share the same room, there's no fear of someone seeing or talking. You can give my reference when discussing. If you feel comfortable and he feels comfortable, then go ahead! Of course, you don't have to roam around announcing what you did."

***

There was a massive explosion in Kalikot in June 2011. A bomb had gone off, and for someone who had barely lived by escaping the thick clouds of smoke, the explosion petrified more. An 11-year-old child got injured while sowing corn in Kalikot district's Phoimahadev.

I had the opportunity to assist in his treatment. Since many had volunteered to help, he got better and his eyes recuperated. We treated the wounds on his face, neck, and hands. The more often I met him, the more I sympathized with his pain.

After he recovered, I reached Phoi searching for his home. It was amid the Pandey settlement.

We were supposed to stay at Yamlal Pandey sir's house. As we were climbing up to reach there, I menstruated. It was already dark when we reached there. The power was out. Outside the house, they had kept a cot where two young girls sat. I was so tired that I nearly threw myself off to the cot. "Sit afar, didi-there!" the girl pattered.

"Are you untouched?" Without waiting for her reply, I added: "Same here. I'll sit here, okay?" I sat on the cot.

She was Yamlal sir's wife who was taking an auxiliary midwifery course in Palpa and had come home during the holidays. The other girl was Yamlal sir's younger sister and studied in ninth grade.

The cowshed we saw when climbing up was an abode for observing menstrual rites in the past. Since the daughter-in-law was newly-wed and college-educated, they had her stay outside but close to home.

They ate outside and slept on that bed, with a thin blanket to cover their body. However, Yamlal sir, his mother, his brother, and I ate together. Rita (from Jumla) and I were given the best beddings and warm blankets, up on the second floor, in the guest room.

There was a latrine in construction. Since going to the thicket was a tortuous affair, I was given the luxury of using the under-construction latrine, which I later did. Early in the morning, Yamlal sir's mother cooked some chapatis made from corn and barley flour. Huddled close to the warm fire, we ate the large and fluffy chapatis, drank milk, and chatted.

Mother said, "If you touch the foundation of a house during menstruation, eat milk-yogurt, step in without observing the five days' ritual, or touch menfolk, it will be a bad omen. The dead ancestors will get mad at us. The gods will be furious." There was nothing new to this story. I tried to persuade her smiling and bid the family goodbye keeping the used menstrual pad in the bag.

***

It was a Saturday.

That day Pancheshwar Cooperative had its annual general meeting. At the end of that program, we were given snacks in their office. Without having those, I went to the neighbor's house, where I met the landlady and her husband as well as their daughter.

"I waited up the entire night with cell phone on my hand. But you didn't call," I said. "Is the cow sick? Or are the kids unwell?"

The husband replied excitingly but shamefaced: "No, sister. Everything's fine."

I explained what had happened to me: "Your wife nearly threw me into the Tila River. I was with your daughters in the kitchen, the day before yesterday. Your wife came suddenly and asked if I'd like some curd. I said yes and started explaining to her my situation. Her face turned blue right away. She was tongue-tied. 'Are you sure you aren't menstruating? she asked.'"

I had reached that kitchen by a mere coincidence. In the hall of the Pancheshwar Cooperative Office, I was discussing the campaign against observing the menstruation rites. It was break time and they served noodles and eggs. I said I would prefer rice instead and wanted to skip the snack because I was a vegetarian. As for the noodles, I didn't feel like eating it, having eaten a lot of instant noodles back in my hostel days. I saw the daughter kneading the dough for the chapatis. I joked around that I was there for breakfast.

She had recently taken her tenth standard exams. The son studied in Khalanga bazaar. I chatted with the daughter and waiting for the chapatis. Since I was in a rush, I started eating. She was cooking eggplants to which I was allergic and I told her I won't take any. At that moment, the wife had arrived. Even though we hadn't talked before, she knew I was the trainer for the program. I too knew her.

"It's been two days," I said.

She paused with the theki (a narrow-mouthed cylindrical wooden tub for churning butter) of curd, a bowl, and a ladle in her hands. "Then I won't give it to you. When my daughter pleaded for curd some days ago, I didn't give it to her either."

[Laughing] "I have been saying that thing is an illusion and it's wrong for a long time at your doorsteps. You know it from your friends, don't you? Things change. They have to. Outdated things must go! Didn't you go to Kathmandu a few days ago and return? Wasn't this road constructed only a while ago? Now you carry a cellphone; the world around you has changed. Look at how you're dressing today and how you did before. One must flow with time. Give the curd to me, I'm getting late. I came here to eat chapatis since I don't eat any eggs." I added the last line in a pleading voice.

"How can you say that? If my cow falls sick and dies, who is to blame?" She scowled.

"We discussed this in yesterday's training. Nothing will happen mother. This is all because of fear, as we've been scared for a long time for nothing," the daughter who was listening to the conversation for a long time said.

"Okay, if you're not giving me the curd, I won't eat the chapati, even though I'm hungry. I won't even go to the training. If your cow is going to fall sick, it should have been by now-because I've already polluted the kitchen. Look, I've touched them, and my soul has already eaten that curd."

She neither spoke nor did she give me the curd.

"If the cow falls sick, I'll take the responsibility, okay? Now give me some of it." I added in a comical tone, "I should've scooped some before."

With some hesitation, she gave me some. I held the bowl of curd, scooped some, and returned it. That was my tactic to touch her theki.

I offered my mobile number gobbling up my food. "I'll be around in Khalanga for a week more. If you or the animals fall sick, please let me know. I'll be here in fifteen minutes. And don't worry about the cost," I said and bid them goodbye.

I was not menstruating that day. Whenever I was in places like gatherings, meetings, programs, or seminars, I always, without hesitation, menstruated. I touched them and their foods exclaiming it was my second day and laughed and sometimes broke them the news after eating. "O god, I had been menstruating. We sat and ate together. I messed things up," I would say and laugh.

2012, Balkot, Arghakhanchi

I set off for the post-funeral rites of my mitini sister's mother. As soon as I got the bus ticket, I felt the gush of blood down there. I, the one, who doesn't stop at it, was to meet with the ones who observe these rites religiously. Obviously, it was a working recipe for ruckus. I chose to go notwithstanding, and arrived on the twelfth day of the mourning (the second last day). Everyone was engaged in the preparation for the thirteen day of weaning.

It was quite a gathering. People from both home and abroad had come. I was particularly glad to see that they had a proper toilet with adequate water. This was luxury for me, for the one who had hidden things in situations graver than this. The tasks to perform too were light. I did what I could and what I knew, and left my 'untouchable' prints everywhere. They might have barred other women from the function if they knew they had been menstruating but I sneaked and barged into the very core of the function without their knowledge.

As usual, nobody fell on the floor with frothy mouths and convulsive bodies. No animals suddenly died the following night. No grandpas and grandmas choked on their food to death. While the sons and daughters of the family talked about how the function went, they said they were content with how everything was managed, how the function was more organized than during the father's demise.

"Yeah, I agree. It was better than last time. But if you had a menstruating woman in kitchen during the father's, it would have been equally good," I said.

"Who're you talking about," my mitini asked.

"Nobody. Just a thought," I said.

A Man Toppled to the Ground

What follows is an incident of a training from Haku, Jumla.

We had come to Haku to understand the impact of our training-whether the participants exercised what they'd learned in theory and to locate any difficult household or area needing further assistance. At the end of the group work, I read out the following rules:

- Form a group of six people, both men and women and come to me.
- The rest, stay quiet and observe. We will reflect on it later.
- I will give you this card (showing the card I had in my hand); don't show it to anyone else. Take a sneak peek.
- Whatever is written on the card, you'll be that. You won't have the role or identity you have now.
- I will read out some sentences. If you like them, take a step forward. If you don't like them or get offended, take a step back. If you feel indifferent to it, stay where you are.

I had made the card in a way that there were all distinct groups, including Brahmins, men, dalits, women, and shamans. The roles they were given often contrasted with what they were. For instance, I had assigned the role of a menstruating woman to a man.

The man who tumbled to the ground was a shaman who used to travel around the village suggesting everyone observe the menstrual rites. That is why my friends had called me there. Upon seeing the card, without even uttering a cry of pain, he fell to the floor fluttering his eyelids. On his card was written: 'A poor menstruating dalit woman.'

We lay him and straightened his head. He got up in a few minutes. Later he confessed: "As soon as I saw the card, I got scared. I didn't exactly know what happened after that."

The moral of the anecdote was-as long as there is fear inside our hearts, we cannot move forward. To progress in life, one needs a pristine and open mind, one that will learn with proper demeanor and faith. With around thirty people on the ground, the informative game targeting shamans as well as elder patriarchs and matriarchs was conducted, hoping to win over their age-old thinking.

I never use computers while training these people. I can engage people who have never been to training and bring them to stimulating discussions, thereby converting almost 80% of them-I can say this with confidence stemming from my experience. But for this, meeting once is not enough. Conversion takes time. I have to stay together, dine together, sing and dance together in their villages as well as reach out to problematic households, creating awareness through participation. Unless you make people feel their own, they won't budge. After all, who wants to be changed by strangers with nothing humane to offer than fancy computer pictures which they call PowerPoint slides?

***

On a downhill trail below the Muktinath Temple

Father could descend downhill slopes easily, while for me climbing uphill was rather easier.

During that descent, my father's face turned bright red as if droplets of blood was about to drip from the skin.

I was getting restless and wanted to talk to him.

"Ba (father), do you know who's the priest here?"

"A woman," he said.

"Did you ask how many were there?"

"Don't know. I didn't ask."

"Did you find how many days the temple's going to be closed?"

"No, why should I ask all these?"

"But I've asked," I said. "The temple has two women priests and they're not Upadhyaya Brahmin but Bhote's daughters. Bhoteni, it is! And this temple never closes. People have kept the sisters, daughters, goddesses in somebody else's cowsheds. Think of what they went through! In reality, those people who treat their daughters and wives as livestock are the sinners. We shouldn't do a ritual? We shouldn't touch the gods? Hogwash!"

When blinded by my anger, as if possessed by some spirits, I didn't realize what I was saying. I suddenly got mad at my elder sisters because none of them revolted against this tradition! None of them even thanked me: heartless breathing goddesses ...

I have asked the gods and goddesses-Tripura, Khàdà Devi, Manakàmanà, and Vindavàsini-not just once but many times. But they don't seem to bother. They didn't forbid me to visit them. I got so upset I posted it in Facebook, about questioning Tripura and Ugratàrà. Still, they weren't furious at me. They did nothing bad.

I also have asked the gods:

"O Gods, O Men, am I allowed in your society? Look, I am menstruating!"

No Gods spoke, not even a word.

***

It was the second day of the training.

We set off to Kudari from Lamra village. The women of Dhimkot, Kudari, although far away from the cities, had made significant strides in transforming the age-old tradition. By the time we had learned the secret of this transformation, it was already midday. We were all starving and exhausted. A woman volunteer, who's been volunteering for twenty-seven years said between mouthfuls: "I've been working for twenty-seven years, but the realization came only yesterday. I never ate in a hotel because menstruating or lower caste women might have touched the food. I rather walked hungry and spent the night without a stomach-soothing morsel," she said. "Sometimes I carried some snacks, while at others I didn't even attend the training. Yesterday, Radha sister said she wouldn't eat if I didn't. Even though she was already at the table, she got up and walked away."

She went on: "She was starving, but she wouldn't touch the food if I didn't. She was on the second day of her menstruation. She had touched the entire hotel. And by the way, I didn't get a toothache by eating food touched by menstruating women. It was because I hadn't cleaned them properly. I'm confident now that nothing will happen."

***

Nothing happened to Mahapandit, the great priest, either. This is an incident from 2004. A resident of Bhandadik, Kaski, Chaturbhuj Paudel is my friend Binita's father. He taught at Nepal Sanskrit University in Dang. He led greater yagyas-religious offerings in a fire-to the Hindu gods.

Chaturbhuj Paudel had come to his daughter's place in Aarubaari. Because I had resigned from my job in Jumla and had been staying in Kathmandu, I went to visit Binita at her residence. Needless to say, I was menstruating. If I hadn't, I might still say I was.

"How are we going to serve your father food?" I asked Binita.

"I'll do it. Then, we can eat later."

"Radha, the curry might get burned. Have a look," she said, busy rolling the dough.

To me, that moment felt like a lottery. I stirred the curry right away, and as always, started working in the kitchen. We served him the food and he ate it with a countenance more in happiness than in remorse. Nothing happened to Mahapandit Buwa.

Menstruation during Puja and Mourning

August 2018 | Ramkot, Kathmandu

My best friend Shanta's mother had just climbed eighty-one. The family decided that they were going to observe a special function called Chaurasi Puja on her behalf (the 84th-year celebration ritual) earlier, because she was old and it would be an excuse to meet with everyone. Her mother had worked hard her entire life. They wanted to dedicate a big happy event for her.

People gathered from all places-Shanta from the United States, I from Chitwan, and others from different places and walks of life.

As soon as I reached home, I menstruated. I stepped downstairs towards mother's room for search of toilet paper. Shanta's mother sat in the middle surrounded by clamoring guests and seemed to be bothered by who had joined the puja and who hadn't. I overheard them but pretended I wasn't. I came to know that some distant relatives too could not attend because they had menstruated in the meantime and were 'unfit' for the rites. On hearing this, Shanta's eyes clashed into mine. I couldn't help but chuckle. "Shanta and I are also menstruating if that's something relevant," I said. "But we chose to come. They didn't want to come and took rescue to menstruation as an excuse."

The ladies stared at us but didn't approach for further engagement.

The next day, the ceremony began. Most of the guests knew I belonged to a 'lower' Brahmin family and because of which I pretended not to like going to the Mool Shanti Puja (a religious mantra-chanting ritual performed to calm down the nakshatras or planets). After all, I didn't want to create a scene in a close friend's public ceremony. Not that I didn't want to intervene-which usually would be the case whether I liked it or not-but because that was Shanta's mother's special day, I stayed afar.

But they called me to the ceremony. I sat with Shanta's mother, sisters, brothers, sisters-in-law, and other members of the family in the sacrificial pavilion. I complied to every ceremonial proceeding the priest chanted and guided and clicked photos with the family. The science held up the denouement again; nothing happened to anyone because of my menstruation.

The reason why these incidents have similar beginning and end though entirely different characters is: I'm testing the age-old, untested hypothesis of 'you get harmed when you touch a menstruating woman' in practice. I've set experiments of various kinds with people of various castes and religions and has properly accounted for any random coincidences. Even though this has not been modeled in randomized control trials using scientific experimental techniques, there's enough science in it to prove the point. We must understand that past traditions might have started for a reason which might be totally irrelevant now. The nostalgia of the past keeps us from marching to the front of both intellectual and societal development.

Thus, I'm stating this time and again to establish, and with evidence, that with enough preliminary data, we can confidently declare that menstruation is absolutely unrelated to doing any harm-just in case for the most religious (not literal) skeptics. Otherwise, to think it would, is itself senseless. Anyone who's committed to science and scientific understanding would see the nature with its spectacles. Menstruation cannot be a problem to them, ever, in any situation-whether they're climbing Everest, performing their kid's rice weaning, or mourning for their parents. Most importantly, we should carry the baton for the sake of people who deserve to be told the truth.

***

When my own mother died, after a long and tiring debate, my sister, brother and I decided to stay in a single room to mourn her death. Binu didi, the eldest, and Usha didi, the third-born, also decided to mourn in the same room but at a distance. The next day my younger sister Samjhana menstruated.

"I'm untouched," she whispered into my ears.

"Okay. So, what are you going to do about it?" I replied. "You should decide for yourself. Being both a medical student and a journalist, you're more than capable of deciding what's best for you. I wouldn't force you for anything but if you ask me, I've stopped doing this for a long time. It's been years."

"What do I do then I can't decide," she said.

"How about getting some menstrual pads and sitting for the mourning? But again, I wouldn't force it."

We asked our neighbor Bandana Ghimire to arrange for her some pads. Disposing them was not a big deal after all. We shared our works amongst the three siblings. There were heaps of work: cleaning the rooms, mud-plastering the floor, bathing, washing, fetching water, arranging for the puja items, among many others. Building an odaan (a tri-legged iron stand for holding pots to cook food), offering prayers, and listening to the Garuda Purana (one of the eighteen Puranas the verses of which are recited starting the fifth day of someone's death) became our daily routine. Apart from doing all these, we talked with the guests who came over to see us and maintained the regularity of the house chores. We cried together when we wanted to. We ate together when it was time. We laughed together at times when we forgot for a fraction of a second that our mother was no more-we'd lost her.

Nothing changed before and after my sister menstruated. It was time-and-again-tested phenomenon-that nothing ever happened or changed either to the state of affairs or someone's health when we participated in religious or social rituals on menstruation. But for others and religious scriptures, it would be different. If you're bleeding, you ought to stay separate. You can neither pray nor sit for the puja. Let alone participating in the mourning of your mother, you couldn't even watch those who mourn, according to those people.

***

I took Priya and Julia to a place called Bijayanagar in Jumla traversing through the districts of Nepalgunj, Bajura, Humla, Mugu and Jumla to the home where I had taken rebirth. It was a place I consider I was re-born as a human again after the Maoist mishap. A boxer dog welcomed us with wining barks that left me doubtful about whether barking dogs seldom bite. Sat in a corner with her usual knitting sweater and a white dhoti wrapped around her waist, meet aama (a mother-like acquaintance befriended according to our universal-humanhood philosophy), Mahashankar Meet buwa's wife, caught our eyes. Her frowning face lighted up a bit after seeing me. She had finished with the fifteenth-day Shraddha ceremony of her husband.

"So, how was it? Did anyone fall ill? I had to visit Bajura so I couldn't come," I said.

"No, everyone's fine. It all ended with peace. I came to understand how popular he was only after his death. There were people from all over," she said.

From Nepal Academy to Pashupatinath, I had touched the dead body of Meet buwa throughout. I had touched his sons. I had offered flowers to his dead body and had entered the cremation house. With that level of digression, something must have happened. I mocked myself.

"I didn't realize there were this many people who admired father," she added.

"Yes, mother. There are certain things we only realize after someone's death. In some way, death un-blinds us, isn't it?" I said. For some reason, I didn't have a chance to disclose the funeral incident of her husband. I should have.

The Servile Gender

“Are you still a nurse?” People who’d read my book Jumla: A Nurse’s Story always asked me. In response, I but smiled and said 'yes'.

I answered: “I specialize in community-based nursing service. My life and education have been hovering around the same. It has everything to do with birth and birthing practices at least on the outside.”

I often recline in solitary in the porch and think about all those babies of whose births I assisted-be it in Gandaki Hospital’s maternity ward or Bharatpur Hospital’s operation theatre, or in Jumla Hospital. They looked the same, were the same. All babies started off by breathing the air around. They cried like I often did. Each time they stepped on this earth, they brought smiles on their mother’s face just enough to forget the pain and suffering, poverty and injustice, without an exception. Each time they were born, they made their mother-who now all in smiles-forget how hard it was for them to grow up as a girl.

I became happier when the child cried than when the mother smiled. The moment new lives sprang to the air outside their mother’s wombs, they instantly cried mostly in short episodic whines and often stuttering and gasping for air. It reminded me of my mother who once gave me a rough field-guide to distinguish whether it’s a girl or a boy from outside the labor room: if a child cries “kaha kaha” (where, where?) as soon as she’s born, she must be a girl as she's asking where she's supposed to go after marriage. And if it is a boy, he cries "yaha yaha" (here, here), which meant "I'm meant to stay here." I've been interested in this acoustic study for long and having been listened to hundreds of baby whines and with little bit of common sense, all I can say is they're not demonstrating any intellectual capability of foreseeing their own future. The philosophy of this kind of truth pursuit is called wild guess. It was a reckless synthesis some older people came up with, years ago.

Of course, they're crying to breathe properly, to kick start their lungs. They're innocent beings who just came out of the peace of the womb to get a glimpse of human classificatory tropes. And no sooner had they done that, they were fallen into baskets of gender stereotypes we've assigned them. We're gender-engineering from the beginning of a child's life and before they realize this is going to be a vicious cycle of transferring these 'traditions' to the next generation, they become one of us. Children won't cry differently when they're born even if men go to their wives' home after marriage: this was my hypocritical reply to my innocent mother who was no more than a role-playing victim.

Girls are emotionally more matured and balanced. But this would be coquettish for the society. Do this; don't do that. Walk like this, not like that-that is typically revealing. Not just they're told how to speak, how to eat, and how to dress, they're also taught to be intellectually inferior to boys. This is a trickier feat to pull off: to make people understand and break the chains of habitual automaticity. Shattering the status quo requires mighty hands and many of them at once. But to deny that there are no chains is more arduous a problem than the unwillingness to break the chains.

The society raises a girl child like we raise black pepper seeds. Pepper seeds in their premature days aspire to test the currents of air and fly far off to alien places, like daughters. They bloom into the green pulps of nectars of vigor and might who easily camouflage with their green leaves, like daughters whose contributions go unnoticed. When she matures, she becomes utilitarian both at her home and in the in-laws'. Her body radiates heat that has to be curtailed somehow. Her sensualistic fervor has to be 'tamed'. Daughters have to be good listeners in order to be good daughters. Lustful eyes eye them in every nook and drag them in their cozy spaces, virtually, all the time. And if unlucky, in real, to the horror of the society.

At the age of six or seven, when she's still frightened by demons in her dream, she has to tame another demon called menstruation. Her natural body response which surprises her all of a sudden one day distracts her to the fullest. At the age of six or seven, she has to deal with exactly the same problem as a mid-aged woman. She's barred from entering into a kitchen and touching the male members of the family.

Don't see your brother, you'll be sinned.

Don't see your father, you'll be damned.

Don't do this; don't do that.

Just don't.

If her brother is small, he will too be confused why her sister is jailed in her own house, if lucky, or in a cow-shed, if unlucky. She'll be inferior than her brother. Her stature now has a short ceiling she's going to find difficult to shatter. She becomes untouchable. No matter how fluent her language is or how savvy she's with computers, she'll still be inferior to her brother. As she grows up, like peppers, she will gradually turn from rich, fruity seed into a brown and wrinkled dot. Her body registers as she grows up marks of humiliation, discrimination, and violence. She will be traumatized inside. She will be fighting her own demons which are mostly invisible to others, especially males. Her curiosity would have been quashed. Her questions are no longer valid. In the same society where a boy is brought up unhindered by any blockades, obstructions and fortifications, to a point in future when he realizes that he is stronger, freer, and un-tied to any restrictions, a girl, on the other hand, is tied by shackles. It is natural to conclude that almost half of the prominent genders-the male-in absence of monthly dos and don'ts, will certainly feel more confident, more assertive, and more convinced that he is supposedly superior. In most cases, a girl can't ever live up to societal expectations of menstrual barricades. She gives up because she's a daughter. She's made to.

Talking of the darker side, one of the evils of our society is that it instigates boys to a path that ultimately leads to violence against its female counterpart. I always compare this with water-soaked pea seeds being prepared for pickles where not just their bodies get festered but also peeled off. Boys can leave their comfort zones and float around on the surface. Meaning-boys are allowed to do whatever they feel is right. They are considered more powerful than their sisters and mothers. This mentality encourages boys to be violent and girls to feel natural standing on the receiving end. This is akin to all geographical areas-from east to west and south to north, across all castes and tropes. Choosing to practice menstrual rites plays a significant role in the socialization of children and the distribution of power, and the society has paid no attention to curb it whatsoever.

The Male Psyche

Patiani, Chitwan

I am the only son of the family. There are around more than thirty women in a closed room and along with them, some school-going children. I intend not to cook food but I have to.

Mother sits by the kitchen's door and is instructing me on the additives that go in the cooking: coil, then salt-yeah, that's just right amount, turmeric-half a spoon or you'll scare the children away, and spices-feel free to add more. I used to hate cooking and would often imagine menstruating so that I wouldn't have to cook every now and then. I am a boy.

But these days, I feel relieved that I don't menstruate. It is from mother and sister's friends that I have known what menstruation is and the dos and the don'ts, and it has made me happy.

I feel luckier and more independent than my sister-a sister who is more educated, could speak English, and use computers. I am the stronger son of the family amongst the weaker daughters, or more emphatically, my sisters. What if sister is elder than me, I am more privileged because she can't touch me and father for several days once every month. But I can. In those days, she can neither enter the kitchen nor touch food. She becomes untouchable, dirty.

I am the most senior member of the family after father. I consider myself as a morally superior, privileged member of the family, a better person, after father. It is not the body but the power I have acquired that gives me the respect.

***

This moral privilege loosens up a bit when it comes to treating his female counterparts, or technically sisters. He beats her up on the watch of his parents. He teases his female friends on the indirect validation of his teachers. As he grows up, he practices this art onto the passers-by and ultimately masters at the art of eve-teasing. The level of power he exercises before marriage makes him feel superior, which then he carries forward after marriage, too. He transforms himself into a domineering husband. This senior human being ultimately becomes a lead of every two-thirds of violent crimes or social evils. He endorses it, organizes it, and turns it into a successful campaign that enables him to sustain power throughout history and contemporaneity. Both temporally and spatially.

He gets swelled up like a pea seed. He retains power in all spheres of life, whether at home, at office, on the way, or at school. Everywhere. In some instances, he perpetuates the culture of violence.

But a sister or daughter of the same family becomes a shrinking pea. Every month when she menstruates, she feels powerless, shrunk to half her dignity. She learns to live an inferior life as compared to her brother who's younger than her, less educated, less experienced. She's made to be different than him, and this makes her detached and uninterested in her studies. She loses to her constant struggle with education and sometimes tastes failure. Her dreams are squashed like sardines together, and some of those dreams find an escape in marriage, either through compulsion of parent's force or being out-of-options. In an attempt of living, she dies every day in agony, repentance, exasperation, and the fear of violence. Like constitutional law is the law of the laws, menstrual discrimination is also the mother of all violent practices inflicted against women.

The argument can be extrapolated to explain the relation of rape and menstruation-related practices. Unless one disengages the cultural shackles that women are in, claiming to stop rape is nothing but feeble palms trying to silhouette the sun. It is unfortunate that neither Nepal government nor non-governmental bodies are engaged in seeking the roots of the problems. Rather, they're relishing on their work on stems, flowers, and fruits.

Whenever I claim things as such, the synthesis of most answers would be: "Our family is not a strict Brahmin family," or "We don't live in Western Nepal, do we?" As if saying so would vanish the actual evil practices prominent in the society. Why are we even talking about this if there are no practices as such? Without wind, leaves don't tear.

Menstrual Rites are Widespread

Both men and women of Majhi community of Ramechhap endorse the practice of menstrual rites. They say their dead ancestors are very strict on this. Irrespective of age, they find it their duty to 'preserve' their culture. The older generation wear nothing inside during menstruation while the newer one stuff old ragged clothes inside the pajamas.

Menstruation is also practiced in Tamang families of Makwanpur, Kavre, Sindhupalchowk, and Kathmandu but in different ways. Even though they preach Buddhism, they do not worship during their menstrual days, and particularly avoid eating sour food. They are more superstitious about the menstrual pads. The practice is more intensely prevalent in hetero-cultural areas where Brahmins, Chhetris, or other orthodox Hindu practitioners live together along with Tamangs.

Newar families too practice menstrual rites; they're rather stricter in this. They don't allow menstruators to touch water taps. Before offering tenants rent in their houses, many of them make sure the renters observe rites the home owners believe should be practiced. It is generally perceived that unlike in Brahmins and Chhetris, because Newari girls stay in gufa (a form of tradition-regulated house-stay; literally, 'in a cave') in the pre-menstrual days, Newars do not have secluding menstrual practices. But you cannot call this an empowerment practice-restricting from seeing a male or the roof-top of a house for 12 consecutive days-or the sunrays. Or being able to eat fish only after bathing, that too after the 6th day, or greasing one's body in oilseed cakes, or eating only on the sixth and twelfth day in the gufa. We can put forward as many positive stories as we can: we allow a friend in the gufa; we keep girls at menarche in groups; we have eased up some restrictions, or even argue that children, of age 9–12, are pleased to be at the gufa, but those are just arguments for the sake of argument. Children under eighteen are not citizens, says World Health Organization. How can we expect them to be mentally and psychologically matured for the act?

If a girl menstruates before she enters the gufa, she has to live in it right then. She is allowed to roam around in the house except the kitchen and worship room. On the twelfth day of her gufa, before she's allowed to see the first rays of the sun, she must watch herself in a copper bowl. To ask daughters to request the Sun, the deity, for a husband like Lord Bishnu as a benediction is not expert advice but squashing the career aspirations of a girl and perpetuating a compulsive culture which every girl has to abide.

If a girl somehow dies in a gufa, what follows is a horrifying custom of digging a hole through the wall and carrying her body to the ground floor to bury her there. However specialized a practice they consider and explain gufa-system as, the girls who dwell in there feel dejected, isolated, and garner a sense of inferiority complex, as seen in many cases.

The custom of practicing menstrual rites is found in Tharu communities, too. Influenced by Bahuns and Chhetris, the Tharu communities of Chitwan, Rupandehi and other districts have started observing menstruation-related customs. Even though they do not strictly observe these customs in their private sphere, or that husbands and wives' beds may be common, they seem to stay away from each other. However, some women cook food by themselves but offer separate oil, salt, and flour to their gods. These Tharu women practice menstrual dos and don'ts in the public sphere only to preserve their 'reputation', as seen in many families.

Similar to Tharus, the Limbu community also restricts women in some cases especially in public life. When I got an opportunity to peek into Madheshi families' private life-that was in 2005-I was dismissed because "oh, isn't it prevalent only in Hill-Brahmins and Chhetris?" On deeper scrutiny, we still find some practices as such though it remains invisible because such affairs are private. Menstruating women, however, still avoid entering the kitchen, worshipping gods, and touching fruits, vegetables and sour foods. When it comes to understanding menstruation and restrictions, the Madheshi community is no different than others.

A long list of don'ts also characterizes the menstruation trends of indigenous communities of Dahakhani in Chitwan district as in other communities.

Similarly, in families with differently able members e.g., in cases of physical disabilities, mothers and sisters form the primary caretakers. Likewise, in intellectually challenged people, undertaking menstrual sanitation and preserving their rights is even more problematic. These members often take their diapers or pads off and, in some instances, chew them, or are forced to live in soiled conditions. They are often physically, mentally, and sexually abused, and in extreme cases forced to undergo a hysterectomy to prevent unwanted pregnancies. This is not only a gross violation of human rights, but also puts them at a higher risk of medical complications.

Regarding transgender communities, they do not observe menstrual practices but have to face problems of other sorts. They cannot express the hormone-related outpouring in their families either intentionally or not, and feel inferior because of not being able to live a sexually active life. As a result, they have to separate from their partners and live by themselves. Worse, they fear ostracism on issues like use of public toilets and the management of menstrual pads.

Menstruation becomes grave a problem especially during disasters. Either during the Koshi flood (2008) or earthquake (2015) or the floods of 2016 and 2017, menstruation remained one of the prominent issues. In most instances, the concerned authorities and the organizations have no knowledge of positioning women's natural necessities as a non-dismissive priority. In other cases, they overlook them due to the lack of fund. But when the authorities take the initiative, they are laughed at the "trivial act of distributing pads" during grave situations and are often mocked.

On the other side, donors too act irresponsibly and focus on restricted priorities, leaving behind a bewildered population who have worn menstrual pads like masks because of ignorance.

***

Three months into the 2015 earthquake, an incident occurred in a place called Sipaghat in Kavre district. In one of the corners of the front yard, a plate and a glass rested upside down on the ground, which reminded me of my childhood.

"Can I have a glass of water, auntie?" I gestured with my wrinkling forehead in exasperation. "The sun is scorching and I'm dying of thirst."

The air was bubbling and boiling. Mercury was at the peak. A family whose house was destroyed had been living there. There was also an office in it. I was on the porch. The woman looked at me for a moment and froze as if she ran out of words. She pointed toward the house innards. "See the brass pot over there? Help yourself out and drink some water, dear," she said.

I knew the drill. But I wanted her to take the test. "So, are you menstruating?" I asked.

"It's been two days," she blushed at the unexpected question.

"Yeah, you're right…about the thing," I reached for my buttock and signaled that I too had menstruated. "I'm also two days into it. But it's not written in your face, is it? Nobody knows. But I drank water from the pot. What now?"

She smiled. The people around also burst into laughter. In fact, there was no option to laughter. That's one way to accept the truth.

Different village but same district and context: there was this girl, eleven or twelve, who stayed home all along sleeping even after schools resumed in the post-earthquake days. I was curious. The school in those days ran on the playground; it was already one week into its opening. The girl, uncombed, wore rugged clothes and chose not to join the gathering. I waited until dinner to dig more. She didn't even appear once under that tarpaulin-roof where we ate. When I reached the point of no return, I had to ask about her.

"She's menstruated for the first time. She's here to hide," a person said.

As she was barred from going to many places, and especially the kitchen, she stood afar and stretched her hand toward the kitchen with an eating plate on it. It was no different than Western Nepal, a place which is stereotyped for such practices.

They poured water from atop which babbled into the glass for a while. She drank it like a camel. Saraswati (the goddess of education)-it was her name-was forced to leave school because she was menarcheal and her family feared she would see or touch her father, who had been a teacher, and her brother, who was a student in the same school.

Superstition aside. I wonder who came up with an argument that you couldn't avoid touching one teacher and one student in a school with hundreds and that for few days. Strange! And what is more depressing is her father who was also a teacher and who was supposed to discourage such practice and not uphold it, not just perpetuated it at her health's cost, but also barred her from various other things. In fact, it is humans, both men and women, who institutionalize superstitious observation of menstrual stupidity. The doors and the windows of the schools aren't interested in who touches them. Books don't complain.

Only humans. And all kinds of humans. They validate them like the texts in their textbooks.

A few girls reach menarcheal age when they are in class four. Both boys and girls would have grasped this idea of what menstruation is at that age, albeit a flawed understanding, from their home. The schools, however, don't teach this to the students at all. There's a whole lot of learning material in both books and curriculum on cleanliness of the entire body and sanitary habits. From habits like bathing and washing hands before eating and after toilet to peeing on pans and not on pants, a lot of things are taught. But they never teach that girls should wash their genitals from front to the back and not the other way round because their vagina might get infected from the germs of the fecal remains in the back. This sanitation habit is more important to girls as compared.

When girls reach class five, the number of them who menstruate is slightly more. But the books have nothing, merely a caption on it. At this stage, girls need at least a basic understanding of menstrual sanitation and pad-how-to, to say the least. Boys too need to learn their role in this; they have to be taught both at school and home about how to take and treat the matter.

In classes six and seven, the learning on menstrual health turns a bit technical and until it reaches class nine, few pages of "Environmental Health and Physical Education" are filled with explicit anatomical sketches of reproductive organs. Most of the girls would have turned fifteen and menstruated and might have a functional understanding of it. Similarly, most of them also would be taught citizen-level role in the society. However, the curriculum doesn't link between the two. When children are promoted to class ten, the available knowledge in books get demoted. There's not an iota of social side of menstruation in it. The schools, on the other side, do not inform the children of these issues but confuse them more. And the media add more confusion to the already-confused state.

We live in the 21st century where most of the homes have means and resources for dignified living. But women still strive for dignified menstruation because most of the families are unaware of it. They either do not want to talk about it or dismiss it during discussion. Most NGOs and INGOs, on the other hand, restrict it only to syllabic-discussion. Women are dying because of unhealthy menstrual practices on the one hand, while on the other, nobody wants to be in the frontline to challenge it directly. Some organizations and people in some cases, as shameful as it sounds, go one step ahead to promote these practices.

Menstrual women are hidden in a different room as explicated in Hindu religious texts so that they wouldn't be able to see the sunrays and the male members of their family. When approached with counter-arguments, most people say that practicing these menstrual beliefs is dictated by religion. I don't understand how it is. Does traumatizing, humiliating, and animalizing your mothers, daughters, and wives a religious practice or simply a crime? Texts which claim to be life doctrines are written hundreds and thousands of years ago and thus rational thinking in many cases cannot be expected from them. Even though they teach way of life, in many cases such as in Manusmriti: verse 4/40, 4/41 and 4/42, Chanakya Niti: verse 6/3, 11/12; and Garuda Puran: verse 6 and 7, menstruation is deemed as impure, unholy. The book of Rishi Panchami is written to explicate the clauses of emancipation should anyone touch a menstruating woman. The government of Nepal has cancelled Rishi Panchami day as a public holiday but it still has to be seen how government punishes those who take a leave that day for its observance.

The misconception that daughters become impure and unholy during menstruation is still prevalent. Because it is dictated by religious scriptures that girls should undergo kanyadan (an auspicious 'giving-away-of-bride' ceremony in which bride's parents officially 'give' and groom's parents 'accept' the bride, authenticated by the chanting of religious Hindu mantras) way before she menstruates, some parents still participate actively in seeking boys for marrying their daughters in their pre-menstrual days giving rise to child marriages. In the past, parents in Western Nepal used to offer deuki or their daughters secretly to a temple in order to garner a lot of pious merit. This practice, called Deuki system, is also dictated by religion. It is easy to marry or offer a physically, psychologically, and sexually immature daughter in the name of religion because she cannot simply tell what's happening to her, let alone what will happen in the days to come.

In Kathmandu, there is a practice amongst the Newar community to deem a girl in her pre-menstrual days as a goddess, the chosen one. For this purpose, a girl who hasn't attained a menarche is chosen-called Kumari, the living goddess. What intrigues me is: how does a Kumari (an unmarried girl) lose her divinity after menstruation? Why can't there be a menstruating Kumari? Kathmandu is indeed the place for intellectuals. Still, why are there no dominant voices who disapprove of this thirteenth century practice publicly? Can virtually anything be institutionalized in the name of religion or culture? Even deeming the process which leads to the birth of human beings as unholy and impure? When Kathmandu points its hypocritical finger towards Madhesh or the Western Nepal, it should realize that under the hood of culture, and on the watch of hundreds of intellectuals, it is institutionalizing a hundreds-of-years-old practice which is not just partial but also trivializing women. The rest of the four fingers point back at it, or more aptly put-us.

***

Toward the end of 2005, as I left for Sarkuwa after interacting with shamans, adolescents, teachers and others, I encountered a temple of Devi Bhagawati on the way. I discovered women were not allowed to enter inside. The locked gate stopped me.

But only until I got hands on the keys.

Not just in Baglung, a temple nearby a bus park in Lalitpur also reads a sign "Women Not Allowed to Enter." In some places, such posters are seen pasted even in areas where they sell worship items, way ahead of the temple gate. When they advertise for the post of temple priests and personnel, they explicitly state "Only Men." I have seen the 'women not allowed' posters even in Army Barracks.

Sabarimala temple in Kerala state of India only allowed devotees inside after an X-ray-to which the Supreme Court of India deemed a discrimination against women and a violation of women's rights. Even after the 2018 verdict, women of all age groups and gender cannot enter inside the temple; the controversy is still in the air as of 2020.

Some of my acquaintances invoke Kamakhya Devi and her temple in the state of Assam in North-eastern India to stress that we respect menstruated women. Kamakhya Devi for me is an incorporeal thing, written by someone else, like they've written in Garuda Purana or Manusmriti for that matter.

Pranamis who consider Krishna as their deity consider themselves orthodoxically religious. Pranami gurus who deliberate all as God-made and God as all-knowing suggest that menstruation should not be stigmatized. But their followers still cannot catch up to them.

***

East Chitwan

I was about to discuss menstruation in a group of 100 where almost 20% of them were men. It was to be held on the pavement of Krishna temple.

I waved a stick on my hand and pointed towards the mass. "I beg your pardon beforehand for discussing something that might offend you...for most of you present here are the age of my elder sisters and mother. If you get angry, you can hit me with this stick or scold me."

In forty-five minutes of what followed-which was the story of my life-I shared with them my intense moments and struggles. Toward the end, I saw some of them wiping their tears with the loose end of the sari and scarves. I escaped their wrath; the stick still stood leaned onto the wall. Instead, they praised my father for he had such a daughter like me, and me, for what a father I had.

Not just Hindus, the problem with other religions is almost the same. Nepali Christians, because they have been converted from Hindus, have openly raised their voices against menstrual malpractices in the public domain. They claim they do not have such practices. But in reality, menstruating Nepali Christian women do not worship God or enter the kitchen. Their perspectives towards sanitation are nevertheless the same.

Likewise, both in born- and converted-Muslims, even though they claim it a Hindu-thing, they're almost similar to Hindus in this regard. Menstruated women do not pray or touch Maulanas and people who've been to the Hajj. But in terms of menstrual healthy habits and knowledge of it, there's no difference between Muslims and non-Muslims.

There's not a single religion which is absolutely good or bad in this arena. But the reference texts which have been written by invoking religion and as a weapon have deemed the entire matter a taboo. It will only affect generations of girls,women and every menstruator down the line.

The Ministry of Women and Woman Commission of Nepal were formed only after the participation of governmental and non-governmental representatives in the Beijing Conference in 1995. It was only after then that there were open discussions about women rights and cases of women who'd been left to die came to the fore. But nobody had yet paid attention to the impacts of a pre-historic process which started along with human life-menstruation-and the know-how of what and how it is.

In 2005, the Supreme Court intervened in this matter and directed the then Ministry of Women to draft the directives to minimize Chhaupadi practice and work on it. But except for those cases for which FIR was filed in the police station, other cases remained as good as non-existent. The directives didn't change an iota in the practice. If all other forms of violence were to be put aside and only menstruation-related deaths reported, thirteen women died in ten years just because they menstruated. The deaths garnered international attention. Until 2016, the Ministry of Education, Health, Drinking Water, and Women could not do much in this regard. In August, 2017, two women died in a month interval whilst in Chhaupadi sheds. When activists Amar Sunar and Hira Singh Thapa from Dailekh, Sashi Basnet and Samjhana Paudel from Chitwan, and I took a combined initiative to file a report in the police station, we failed. And this was neither the first time nor the last.

Laws Too Sketchy

On 16 October, 2017, Nepal government drafted "The National Penal (Code) Act 2017," effective from 17 August, 2018, in which sub-sections (3) and (4) of section 168 explicitly talks about menstruation-related offences. The act deems secluding a woman during menstruation or delivery to Chhaupadi sheds or subjecting her to any such acts of discrimination, untouchability, or inhumanity a criminal offence. A person committing such an offence shall be liable to imprisonment up to three months, or a fine of up to Rs. 3000, or both.

But this act is prejudiced, incomplete, and deficient. The fact that the word Chhaupadi is used without properly defining it makes it exclusively a problem of Western Nepal, as if it is non-existent in other parts of the country. It is also mute on who, how, and where to register a complaint if such an act is to be exercised. That clause is like elephant's displaying teeth; they're just there for the sake of existence. It is yet to be seen how the act paves a milestone in incorporating the right to dignified living of menstruating girl or women as guaranteed by the constitution.

I have worked as a volunteer under the leadership of Ministry of Water Supply and under coordination of Ministry of Health, Education, and Women in the Drafting Committee comprised of a group of experts, in 2017. The committee had drafted a policy for dignified menstruation which is still not formulated into an act yet.

There have been people, especially women in the topmost tiers of the state: as president and speaker of the house-or the prime minister, who've turned a deaf ear to the issue of dignified menstruation and have since pitching peace, human rights, empowerment, and sustainable development goals, to the dismay of the affected ones. It shows their lack of compassion toward the victims and the fact that without achieving dignified menstruation, attaining any of those long-term goals is impossible.

There are several evidences to this indifference. For instance-it is clarified by the Reproductive Health Act, 2017, the Strategies by Ministry of Women, 2016, and the 'Manifesto of Dignified Menstruation' observed for the first time in history by the Ministry of Water Supply. The majority of state and non-state actors have taken exclusively to the dirty sheds and filthy pads as their activism and acted as spokespersons for the donor agencies, an act condemnable in itself. It is because of these actions that all reports on menstruation have numbed in constricted definition of traditional malpractice, a few-words' linguistic euphemism which hits the plate but doesn't hit the target.

However, the constitution of Nepal, 2015 from its preamble to almost ten articles unambiguously establish and guarantee dignified menstruation. Article 16-Right to Dignified living; Article 30-Right to Clean Environment; Article 18-Right to Equality; Article 24-Right against Untouchability and Discrimination; Article 36-Right to Food; Article 37-Right to Housing; and Article 38-Rights of Women, resonate with dignified menstruation and other articles of the constitution directly and indirectly.

Manifestoes of none of the political parties who've framed the federal structure to materialize the constitutional promises have prioritized dignified menstruation.

Indeed, as far-reaching as it is, the local, national, and international bodies that have been set up to assist the government have also silenced themselves in the issue of dignified menstruation. Despite menstruation has been a subject of discussion since 2014, it has been limited to water supply, toilets, and menstrual pads. The participation of Nepal in the United Nations programs is also extensive; however, neither it has been successful in appropriating international agendas for local benefits nor been able to set examples for others. It's already evident from the exercise of menstruation-related discourse and actions in the country and its participation abroad. People who advocate openly about menstruation have been shamed and subjected to humiliation through a myriad of physical and electronic means in order to discourage them.

Convention on the Elimination of All Forms of Discrimination against Women (CEDAW) has discouraged menstruation through electronic means in a number of instances. Yet, it has categorized menstruation under 'traditional harmful practices' and stayed silent on menstruation in Sustainable Development Goals, 2030.

The rich and elite women activists and campaigners pay no heed to the fact that menstruation is a universal human phenomenon, and there are associated taboo practices in all kinds of society. This is a blazing example of discouragement or indifference. The non-governmental organizations of Nepal have campaigned exclusively on toilet constructions and partially done so without addressing the needs of menstruating women such as soap, water, waste bins, appropriate changing places, and the availability of menstrual items. They have institutionalized and further entrenched such practices. These actions cannot guarantee a woman's right to a dignified life.

Those who have been working and conducting seminars and workshops on eliminating Chhaupadi or advocating women rights and empowerment are found to have themselves observed menstrual discrimnation. In this regard, it wouldn't be an exaggeration if we say that all the time and money that has been spent is squandered.

***

Okay,

So, do we still have menstrual discrimination at home? What are the ways ahead?

These were the questions I asked in the collective release of the book Dignified Menstruation: Everyone's Business amongst a hundred participants in Boston International College, Bharatpur, Chitwan.

"This is a question better suited to girls," a boy said chuckling.

"Do you do it in your home?" I asked.

"Not here. It's in Deuba's village (president of Nepali Congress Party and prime minister)," someone snapped from the crowd.

"No, it's only in Achham district," another said.

"Isn't it in Humla…or Jumla?"

What I sensed from their answers, or technically questions, was that menstrual practices are Chhaupadi practices, and observed only in Western Nepal.

"Why do you think so? Why only in Deuba's village… or in Achham district do you think? Are you sure?" I said.

What followed was acoustically feeble but thematically legible answer.

In unison:

"I heard it over the radio."

"The newspapers wrote."

"In one story…girl died of snake bite. Isn't that that?"

"No. We don't have Chhaupadi."

"Thank you," I said, with a smile. "Who cooks food when your mother menstruates?" I pointed to the ones whose voices were the loudest.

"I do," a boy said.

"We don't allow mothers and sisters to work during menstruation. They need to rest, right?" the others said.

I turned toward a group of girls and asked, "Where do you sleep during menstruation?"

"Next room…or another bed," they said.

"Where do you eat?"

"Somewhere separate."

"Do you touch your father…or brother?"

"No."

The list was on. Their understanding was: menstrual blood was impure and dirty so they have to observe its rites. Even though they won't lay out the practices in public, they comply with these practices at home.

***

It was early 2013. I got the opportunity to participate in an interaction program organized by Padmakanya Campus in association with the Korean Embassy. After politician and advocate Pushpa Bhusal gave her presentation-the gist of which was menstruation was an exclusively Western-Nepal phenomenon, I questioned how and why it was so in public. It didn't end well.

***

In 2013, delegates from UN Women, Home Ministry, and the German mission represented Nepal in a workshop on women's role in peace, held in Philippines. I was dominated in the midst of the workshop. "What Radha is referring to is practiced only in Western Nepal, which by now has minimized." This was what they had to say.

Similarly, in the same year in Kavre district, where prominent journalists, members of the parliament, constitutional experts, political commentators, and others were present, I was alleged on my face that it was not a problem, that there was a 'scientific' backing to this practice, and that I was perpetuating negativities.

Not just among people, the primary-level school curriculum, specifically subjects such as Social Studies, overtly states that Chhaupadi is an exclusive predicament of Western Nepal. This is nothing but seeding blatant lies into the young minds who will carry it into their adulthood and propagate the same discourse, feeding into a vicious cycle.

Likewise, when it comes to media, the reportage seems to be only when there's a story on Chhau-sheds or about the programs funded by NGOs. Most of other genuine cases remain unreported. Even if they make it to the headlines, the news is either in the nth page, or scribbled superficially without any investigation.

Those who like to call themselves feminists have chosen to keep mum even when dozens of daughters are dying in sheds, preaching peace through silence instead of peace through action. Even if they act, they weave declamatory speeches in seminars or preach peace through social media, if at all; or worse, turn their back on the issue. The other groups advocating women's right-to-their-bodies have paid no heed to menstruation as if it is an extraneous process not originating in woman's body.

Some experts have deemed menstruation as rather personal, individual, or cultural thing. They claim to know the 'scientific' reasons behind observing such practices. They even invoke the argument of right-to-choice and endorse confirming to the menstrual discrimination. Some politicians, as ironical as it sounds, dismiss the entire argument claiming their precious time. "We already have enough problems to handle and menstruation is not one of them. Stop wasting our time and your money by inviting to such trivial events."

These examples are only the tip of the iceberg. The educated, rich, elite politicians, journalists, and activists take menstrual exploitation in women as an everyday conventional occurrence. They get alarmed only when women are forced out of the house to live in a shed. What goes inside is absolutely in the personal space. What's private cannot therefore be made public, for them. What's in the Western Nepal, is not in Eastern, Central, or Mid- or Far-Western. It is for them a geographically isolated beast that has to be conquered, and in some cases, has already been anesthetized. Thus, dismissal is the new trend when it comes to menstruation.

Not just that they don't talk about it, they discourage others who do it. You're disreputable. You're shameless. You talk ill of our religion. You're a foreign agent. Their understanding is that I deserve these titles. My understanding is that they neither understand the problems of universally prevalent menstruation practices nor they intended to understand it. I am not trying to be apologetic or defensive here but listing all comments I garnered would make a multi-volume serial of books.

To nobody's surprise, this is actually a problem of girls and women all over the world. It is enough that several generations of women have borne the brunt of the ignorance, discrimination, and violence inflicted against them. My intention is not to see this anymore and to let the younger generations live the life they want, free from any sort of restriction, discrimination, and violence, either self-imposed or wreaked by the society. This dream has kept me going and will continue to do so in the future.

After hundreds of discussions, debates, and talks, and an inside-out analysis of aspects of menstruation for seven years, I have to say with a heavy heart that the lingering question still remains what are good and bad practices. I have walked a solitary journey of volunteering in the mission of evidence-based advocacy through theoretical and pragmatic dissection. One of the primary aspects of menstruation that ties it with religion is a long list of prohibitions-more than forty of them participatory in nature-that a girl or woman should abide by, and which deems the blood they bear, clothes they wear, items they touch, food they eat, and place they live, impure and unholy. Both Western Nepal and other parts have prohibiting restrictions, though selective and of varying degrees, on girls and women regarding the touching and consumption of food and religious offerings. Things have loosened up no doubt: in many areas they allow menstruating women to eat vegetables and in case of Nepalis living abroad, the restrictions are much looser, but not totally absent. They still do not consume fruits and vegetables they have grown even if they eat bought ones.

From Sanigau's Sheds to Far Overseas

I was awarded with the title of Woman Peace Maker in 2012. During my three months stay in the United States, mostly in several parts of California, and on top of that engaging in eight different discussion sessions with Nepalis, I came to the conclusion that even though they're mingled in a foreign culture and religion, American-born Nepali daughters have been observing prohibiting menstruation practices in their own way. Their colloquial code for this was 'red dot,' or I've been reddened. It took me a while to catch up.

Likewise, during my two months stay in England, I got the opportunity to engage in six formal discussions where we focused on menstruation-related issues. British Nepali practice was no different than the US's. "Barma gaye pani karma sangai," they said to substantiate their practices. It meant "no matter where you go, your customs go with you." Women in their old age came to me, embraced, and said, "even after all the troubles we had back home, it's no different here."

If you're denied eating and touching food items, it is the denial of human rights; it is a state of peace in distress. In a study conducted in the girls of Jumla and Kalikot, girls reported that living through the menstrual days instigated suicidal tendencies in them. These practices seem to be common in Western Nepal, but they're everywhere in different shapes and form. On closer scrutiny, one finds that there is widespread denial of women and human rights in the name of barring certain acts during menstruation. The nature of the problem seems to be different but this difference in practices across various geographical regions is only spatial in nature: girls might stay in separate homes, Chhaupadi sheds, ground floors, animal sheds, separate rooms, separate flats, hotels, in the neighbor's, in the corner where single room is available, under the tarpaulins, and so on, but what's common is they're treated differently, inhumanly, not as an equal.

I too have stayed in the shed in a place called Sanigau, in Jumla district. It was the month of Poush (December-January) and the air outside was chilling. Rain drops pitter-pattered and forecasted snow. The family of home owner slept in second or third story, I'm not sure. Dogs barked on the top of their lungs. I scanned around the dry shed with no sign of human being. The toilet rested almost 100 meters far from the shed, on the other side. Soap and water were unimaginable. The shed was stuffed with stacks of hay, chaff of lentils, and things barely recognizable due to the mist of dust on them. I could hardly find a place to stand but managed to clear off a tiny ground just to accommodate my body. As I lay on the ground on my sleeping bag, the floor which I thought was smooth revealed itself in rather unpleasing manner. My body attracted the invisible insects hidden in the haystacks. They tried their best to enter into my ears and nose. The air reeked of animal fodder, dust, hay, and chaff and stung my nose. I closed my eyes for long enough so my sleepy brain would take over my body.

But instead, my body took over my brain and didn't let it sleep the entire night. I couldn't imagine how I'd pull myself through the night if I had to do it frequently on my own.

***

Central Britain

I couldn't make anything of a 4-year-old crying girl for a long time. I decided to ask. Her sister Sapana (stand-in name) was isolated in a room because she had reached menarche and was barred from entering the kitchen and worship room. The poor girl had been sent for few days in her uncle's house because she would touch her elder sister and run all over the house 'defiling' everything. She had missed her sister so badly when she returned home after few days, she cried and threw tantrums to meet her. She couldn't understand what had suddenly happened or what her sister had done to lock her up like that. Nobody could convince her to content.

There are several things that are factored in shaping the culture or behavior of a person but environment remains one of the most prominent. Environment is what lies around you, everything from living to non-living. Kathmandu does not have menstruation sheds because the living cost is high and you cannot afford to have sheds when you don't have enough space for your homes. In many cases, a different home or room is either unaffordable or hardly practical because of sustenance issues. So, girls and women are cornered to a room and isolated.

However, in districts in Western Nepal like Achham and Bajura, there are plenty of lands for distant accommodation of menstruating daughters. Most of the households have cow sheds. This is one of the ways by which problems of similar nature might exhibit themselves in a myriad of ways. In some destitute families, especially those of Dalits who do not possess any land, they build tiny huts separate from their houses where women have to stay in groups. Whereas in Jumla and Kalikot districts, they build a single house for common usage because of lack of space. They stuff the ground floor with haystacks to warm the room and keep animals in there. When women menstruate, they're made to stay with these animals in the same room. Some families even build separate rooms for isolating menstruating women during the construction of their houses. In a four-storied grandiosity of their homes, they construct a "chhuikullo" (a temporary space for isolation of menstruating girls) to systematically seclude their female members.

Irrespective of differences in geography, economic status, and beliefs, the sole understanding behind such practices is the impurity and unholy-ness of menstrual blood, while the inherent principle remains to socially seclude women from families and parts of the house. In principle, women might not be sent away from home-an exception; however, banning from eating certain foods, touching certain things, and participating in certain events are universal. Whether it is Sapana from England or Asmita from Western Nepal, the underlying motive and nature of the malpractice is similar. Despite that the latter who has nothing but poverty stays in a shed, while the former who can afford a separate room in a bungalow, when they are thirsty, they are not allowed go to their kitchen and fetch water, or touch male members of their families. The constitutional rights imparting equal privilege is outright rejected to them, violated. What's more astonishing is no one gets offended through this practice. The society's psychological machinery is so apt and efficient in convincing women for compliance that most of them do not see this as a violation of their right or even take it as a discomfiture. They're expected to feel at ease; be happy with what they've achieved; and feel proud of being a member of matured women. They're made to believe that they're contributing to preserving culture by all means. This is an ingrained prejudice implanted collectively by patriarchal belief system and aggravated by ignorance. It is daunting a task to question yourself and challenge your own beliefs. To understand how one's own prejudices work does not come natural to most of the people.

The practice of evicting women to sheds are prevalent in twenty-one districts of Nepal namely the erstwhile Far- and Mid-Western region, and includes the Himalayan regions of Gorkha and Dhading districts. Some of the governmental and non-governmental programs in some districts of Far- and Mid-Western regions destroyed animal sheds and declared the districts Chhaupadi-free without demolishing the mental anxiety and Chhau-sheds. This mere tokenism was exercised under the hood of some monetary assistance which obviously did not shake the malpractice in the region.

During Maoist insurgency, the rebel leaders and others destroyed several Chhaupadi sheds and tried to bring the practice to a minimum. But later, they themselves started falling prey to the practice and couldn't avoid observing. They stayed under the protection of tarpaulins, interlaced bamboo-stripped rain covers, and plastic and hay-roofed airy structures. They spent their nights during the difficult days of cold, rain, and snow. The others had homes built for their women. No matter where women stayed, if they're separated from their homes, that's discriminatory. That's human right violation.

Practicing menstruation rites has its roots in the early development of human civilization. In ancient times, menstruation was associated with both positive and negative connotations while in the medieval age it was mostly negative or associated with religion or purity. Because it has been safeguarded with such entrenched beliefs, discrimination in the name of menstruation, and most importantly gender discrimination, has also become intricately complicated.

When people curl their lips in scornful disdain, it is understandable that menstruation is not a priority for them. Even though it is, in reality, they can't say it enough. To make things simple, if we look at it as human rights, the eternal labyrinthine debate of tradition versus laws would be apparently straightforward. Of course, for this to work, we need to be on the same page, willing to consider women's rights as human rights.

Change Intractable but Not Impossible

It is indeed difficult to change something deeply entrenched in the society. Especially when people who train women all day about how these practices curtail their freedom join the sheds like others in the evening. To bring about change is not easy. And to bring about change in someone is even more grueling. It is again stupendously foolish to change something by simply importing foreign content and displaying translated texts and images on PowerPoint slides on a computer through projector. Do we really believe that changing a systematic practice which induces fear, dread, faith, and orthodoxy-easily evoked and deeply entrenched in the minds of people-is just a piece of cake? Can change just come like that?

We should invoke the relationship between nature and science while discussing the issues and in a way people understand and want to listen. Furthermore, we should encourage assimilation through participation and dismantle all negative connotations, practices, and myths first. After all, we intend to live as humans and not animals. There are few things to consider. First-women need some basis of sustenance, and second-they need to look through scientific thinking and alternatives. With these in place, they will be empowered enough to lead the front of independence i.e., stop practicing what doesn't make sense and preach the same to the others. It might take an entire day in order to just elicit a yes from women but it will take weeks or months for them to materialize what they've learnt by self-testing or preach the same in public. All we should develop is patience but only after a good day's work. And not just work but efficient work. The change should be quantifiable, for example-change during the tika ritual during Dashain festival or entry to the temples and not merely ayes, nods, and yeses.

***

When change happened in one family, I became as happy as when it happened in a village. There were several instances in which I felt progress was being made and not everything was futile.

It was second day into the training in Lamjung district. A Care Nepal employee from Ramechhap complained early in the morning. "You know didi I'm thankful to you."

"Thankful for what?" I asked.

"When I left for my residence yesterday, I felt terrible with guilt."

"Really? What was bothering you?"

"Despite being a student of science, I never talked with my parents and sisters about menstrual practices," he said as he lighted up with joy. "Now that I'm married, I should've talked with my wife to stop these Chhui practices. But we'd been playing by the traditional rules… until yesterday when you opened my eyes to the truth… realization-I'd rather say. Thank you, didi."

As I said, one at a time.

In another incident, in the midst of Dashain festival, I got a call from an unknown number. It was a woman from Madi of Chitwan district. "Hello didi, I menstruated in the midst of Dashain tika but I remembered you and chose not to stop there and so I did everything as if normal and I'm calling just to tell you that," she gabbled in a rush.

"Is it? I'm so happy you embraced the truth," I said.

I had met her one evening in 2017 during the construction of houses destroyed by flood. She had two daughters and a business which was doing fairly well. Her daughters were in school and she was determined to give them the best she could.

When a chain breaks somewhere, it initiates the breakage of chains everywhere.

Though not that fast, one at a time.

But stories like this are not always guaranteed to come true at your doorstep. Some people accuse you of outrageous, silly things that are baseless and engage in a fight. There are also women who don't like to sit for trainings and discussions. Even if they do, they show as if they felt inferior. However, they constitute almost only 20% of the willing population. But it really comes as a surprise when people from political parties and the ones who organize women empowerment programs protest against you. And it sometimes feels depressing due to a section of women who complain in public places that we humiliated and scorned them with trivial and reprimanding teachings.

The good news is: when you build trust in people and cultivate personal relationships, they slowly turn their hearts and minds in and even convince others to do so. One, two, three, and more: the numbers keep on rising; voices keep on soaring. It can be taken as a post-awareness transformation and, more importantly, empowerment. When women in every nook are empowered, the village awakens unanimously to declare itself malpractice-free. Neither you've to use a lot of cash for that nor superior authority.

When we kindle the fire of awareness in men and women, we truly succeed in campaigning with long-term repercussions. Makeshift campaigns such as asking for their participation in pointless dialogues or forcibly yoking decisions to their shoulders might do well to some organizations but never to women. Girls will still be in sheds. If we do things in the name of doing things, girls and women will continue to die in the name of upholding the tradition.

Success rates are generally higher when there are mixed communities in a society. Villages have been declared as Chhui-free in as less as six months. For instance-Dillichaur, Kudari Jumla of Jumla district, and Rachuli of Kalikot district can be taken as models. It is also seen that transformation is lackadaisical where Brahmin and Dalit communities live together. Lamragau of Jumla can be an example.

Some people choose to abide by menstrual malpractices in both their private and public lives while some do so only in private. When it comes to Tamang community, they practice under pressure from power players or for 'reputation', sometimes in public institutions like local-level governmental wards. Similarly, employees of NGOs, health workers, teachers, activists, and others practice menstruation-related rites privately in the name of religion, culture, and sometimes catering to in-laws.

It was poverty because of which Asmita and her family ignored the issues of human rights and were fixated on subsistence. Just because she was born a daughter, she had to face self-disgust, dejection, and discrimination from the beginning. She menstruated in her class bench when she was eleven. She realized only after her friends told her. Barred from going to school for 15 days because she was a first-timer, she became an outsider in her own home. The fact did not matter that her father was an educated political leader of the village, though he had lost the election.

In her subsequent bleeding, Asmita wouldn't go to school even when her family members insisted. Some days she did, but didn't stay until the end. There was always something that she remembered at school to avoid classes. She made excuses of all kinds: most of the times, she would feign abdominal pain, at other times her stuffed cloth would be completely soaked in blood and she wouldn't have any extra on her. Sometimes, the cloth would accidently fall in the toilet's hole. She thought it was convenient. Her friends too wouldn't go to school for at least three to five days. They would have their own stories.

Asmita consistently ranked amongst top five students in her fifth standard. But when she was promoted to class six, she fell behind and dropped to the top ten list. Everyone was shocked to see her deteriorate in her studies. But nobody bothered to find the root cause. Class six was slightly difficult than class five but she was a student who liked math and science from her early childhood. All of a sudden, she started to dread those subjects.

It is not that she did not try; she did. But she was lost in the discourse of her parents, friends, and teachers and ran away from responsibility more often. Once a promising student who used to keep her heads up, she now vanished in the crowd of her friends and teachers. More often than not, she'd keep silent in the class. And a time came when a subject that she had been vanquishing vanquished her. She failed in Math. Her dream of becoming an education intellectual like her father was squashing in front of her. No matter how much she tried to bring herself back in the game, she could not spring to her erstwhile position because of absentees and distraction. She became so preoccupied with the stuffed ghost in her groins that it constantly reminded her of whether it was wet, leaking, or worst-if it's still there.

There's a toilet in the school but without water and suits only the boys. It was built by the monetary support of an NGO which bore 60% of the budget. The rest was borne by the local community. No sooner than six months after it was built, it stopped flushing the feces. Locals suspect it was built in the least price possible. All the dirt comes from the upstream, everyone says.

Few other girls like Asmita have left school for good. Some of them are married by their families. These were the girls who experienced sudden deterioration in their studies. The families suspected academic lackluster but the culprit was different: absenteeism due to menstruation. If Asmita missed at least three days a month, she missed 12-fold more annually i.e., 36 days. Some girls miss as many as five days i.e., two months in a year. Add in all the public and casual holidays Nepali schools grant and they'll get the least school time to catch up, not to forget all they have to bear throughout, for just being a daughter.

It is indeed difficult to be born as a daughter. Next time you see a daughter excel in her studies or sports or any other activity, instead of taking credits or contemplating because of who it was possible, keep in mind daughters succeed despite society, not because of it.

The worse Asmita's studies got, the more she was discouraged and frustrated in life. The day before, she was a student who stood in the top five in class. The next day, she failed a subject. The year that followed, she embraced her ultimate fate: marriage, eloped with a guy, and planted the seed of the vicious cycle to continue. Neither she's allowed to return back to her paternal home, nor can she go to Kathmandu which the boy had promised would take her. Her husband has discontinued his studies and wants her to do the same. He sits by the bed all day and bickers with her.

"My menstruation has stopped," she told her husband one day, smiling.

"What? Don't tell me. Do whatever to raise the child. I'm going to India."

She was short on dietary nutrition from the beginning. Her grandmother barred her from eating dairy products. Friends suggested not to eat fruits, as their parents would have suggested to them. She thought she should also uphold the (il)logical barring and avoided all kinds of citrus fruits. Not because she didn't want to eat but because she thought it would offend the family's tribal god.

"I gleamed like a flower in the past. Cheeks were reddened, chubby and smooth. Now…I don't recognize myself…I've lost weight," she says. "Yeah, I get it. My body is donating huge amount of blood to nobody. I think

I'm starving. Poor me, which life's curse am I living?" This is Asmita now.

Such an unlucky girl I am, she says. There were times when Asmita and her brother cuddled together with mother. Those were the good times. Her brother still enjoys the privilege of all the love. He never had to sleep amongst the dirt. But she assuages herself for not having to sleep in cow sheds amongst dung, hay, and creepy insects like her friends, nor wake up in the middle of the night and watch out for mice mischiefs-which could well be ill-intentioned people drooling in lust. From the stories her friend told, she knows that whilst in a shed, the strange shuffling thumps outside can make a lonely girl suspect men climbing the staircase.

She never would have been happy sleeping in a barn. Nobody gets a good night's sleep there, she knows. From the cold air outside to cold dreams-nothing favors a girl in a shed. The biggest fear is the urge to go to a latrine: there wasn't one. No water. No friends. No light. No normal humans could have lived the life Lalsaara and Tulsa lived. They died in a shed from snake bite. Their death was absolutely avoidable.

When a snake bites a girl in the barn, it's different than when it bites a man. When you're bitten, first-you might die without knowing. Second-you're alone in a barn and you'd be dead by the time the others wake up and arrive. Third-when a girl is bitten in a barn, the speed with which the health workers respond is different. If they know you're menstruating, they won't even touch you. Tulsa had to go through all these before she foamed in her mouth and died. When nobody was there to touch her, she cried and called for mother. "Mother, please save me. I don't want to die."

Her cry had echoed into everyone's ears. It is unimaginable how her mother who gave birth to her orphaned would have felt seeing her die in front of her eyes. Or rather, it is unimaginable how she should have felt: she gave birth to an orphaned child, raised her, sent her to the barn one day, and got her killed.

Worse, some people even consider the death of a daughter as averting a disaster. Death of a daughter, death of disgrace, they say.

Is it exactly like that? Turns out, yes for them. To raise a daughter-your own child-and send her to a desolated place where people can easily die because of some stupid tradition-is as good as offering her a death bed. Ironically and literally. But one should only blame the mother after knowing neither the brother who studied in Kathmandu nor the one who was working in India stopped her.

***

I heard someone screaming and looked out of the window. Long screech, probably from a mid-aged woman. They had held something with tweezers and were shouting. Maggots, maggots. I thought it was the fall armyworm which infested the maize plant. She was shouting at the top of her lungs and ravaging the silence of the health post. The nurse gave her a pain killer.

She could have died that day. The ultimate fate reserved for humans is death, no doubt. Some people die of heat stroke. Some die of hypothermia. Others die natural death. I must say these are deaths caused by extraneous reasons. Dying of maggots that you contracted from a horrendously soiled place and which entered your vagina because of some ridiculous tradition you practiced, however, is different. It is different in that it is a consensual act. We, women, consent to being sent to this hell. There are 'tangible' people who send us there. They are giving us a potentially poisoning death-recipe. And we savor on its taste. What else can it be if not it? Who was responsible for the maggots, maggots or men?

Why do we have to follow everything that our elders say, even if it doesn't make any sense (is stupid), is unscientific, and doesn't resonate with the rational teachings of books, radios, logic, and rationality? Did the radio play foul on your psychology? Is it telling a lie? Is this a lie?

Background music:

Son: Father! Mother! I need to share something. Would you come and sit here for a while?

Mother: (scoffs) What are they teaching you at school, kid?

Father: No, it's alright. We had no schooling opportunity. We turned out just fine though ignorant and illiterate.

Son: We discussed on menstruation at school today. Many sirs and madams from Ministry of Women had come. I've called you because they'd told me to share with parents.

Mother: My god! What is happening in schools these days?

Son: Good things for sure, mother. What else can happen? We sat together in school for discussion. You know what? I didn't know that menstrual blood was pure.

Mother: Are you out of your mind? What are you even saying?

Son: It's true, mother. They taught us everything. How can the blood that gave birth to me be impure? Am I impure? I think I'm pretty much convinced now. People don't understand...and it is wrong that sisters are sent to barns and sheds. It's even illegal...you will be punished.

Mother: What punished? Who will punish us?

Son: The government...you can go to jail for three months or be fined three thousand rupees. Or even both.

Father: Do you hear that budi? I don't know about you but I don't want to go to jail. Now if you go to the barns and sheds from now on, I will jail you (laughter). Let's eat together from now on.

Son: Wow, I hadn't expected a happy ending so soon. I'll tell everyone in school tomorrow that my parents have changed their minds. My home is free of menstrual discrimination. And most importantly, nobody has to go to jail from my family.

The music amplifies and the conversation fades for a while.

Commentator: If everything is just right, the baby is held in the inner lining of the uterus. If not, the lining rich in tissues and blood vessels ruptures and sheds off. This collection of tissues and blood which flows is called menstruation. If a woman gets pregnant, she needs rich pure blood to nourish the baby (fetus). Discriminating against women and considering her inferior, untouchable, and full of disdain is a punishable offense. Report these people to the authorities. They will be punished according to the law.

Music resumes.

We all admit it is not as easy as radio dramas. But this is the truth. This is a favorable outcome we should strive for.

***

My own story is no less dreadful than Asmita's. In that sense, I'm the spokesperson for Asmita and thousands of others whose stories are exactly like her, like me, different only in form, space, and time but essentially the same. Asmita's story is my story, your story, and our nation's story:

I felt controlled in my own home. When I was hungry and could not eat what I wanted to eat, was thirsty and could not drink when I wanted to drink, wanted to participate with the family in dinner but was barred from it, longed for a good night's sleep but never got it, loved to go to school but wasn't allowed-nobody knew how hurt I was or how much I cried. They didn't care whether I was still living or had already died. Nobody knew why I kept strolling on cliffs and slopes in isolation choosing death over life. How I pulled through I don't exactly remember but it was living death each day and not dying. I hid the tormented soul with a smiling façade. I had to go through all this just because I was born a daughter; nobody took me seriously, only for granted.

When my health deteriorated and I felt like doing nothing, I left studies. Then I married. I became fragile and home to multiple diseases. I have had intense medical needs but no job or skill. Just because I was barred from trivial things-like sleeping in my own bed, eating whenever I felt-which for me were privileges. I was economically devastated, forever.

Because of this, I could not participate in world-changing frontiers nor could I become a prominent member of society. I was not let to. But I understand the futility of expecting from those who didn't let you to your own kitchen will let you march forward. How could a woman who's not allowed to fetch water when thirsty would be allowed in world-changing forums? Really? How many examples can we think of?

All violence against women inflicted because of being born in that gender point towards menstruation. On surface, it might look as common sense to abide by customs that have been there for thousands of years. These are some of the justifications people evoke in defence:

If that hadn't been true, they wouldn't do it.

That is our culture.

I was born to play the role, why hesitate?

God did this, who's to change?

Ignorance and fatalism are two biggest hurdles which chain human progress. Ignorance is no longer a bliss; it's a lag, a pale painting which needs more vibrant colors. The days are gone when not knowing could land you as a better human being than knowing. Knowing things-more precisely, being well-informed of the truth puts you at a better vantage point to decide for yourself. In case of Asmita and thousands of other girls and women, ignorance, fatalism, and the patriarchal machinery have joined hands together against the feeble opponent who fell victim to taken-for-granted things, superstitions, and (ill)traditions. This is a systematic malpractice that squashes thousands, no millions of dreams. The one who gets the ill in it wouldn't want to get the ill through. The ones who do not get it, the minds and hearts that are yet to sink in, feel weak from the early childhood which will be socialized through as common sense and will be taken for granted. This promotes entrenchment of women in the same pit as they were in, are in, and if the status quo is upheld, will be in. Most of us will be left out in a deep dark well unable to get out in the real world which has only two rescues: either grow crawling nails or somebody rescues you out.

Many lives have been ruined, to say the least. Dreams have wrung, stuttered on their way to realization. The society has debilitated and empowered women at the same time from their early childhood through the intricate socialization channels owing to which girls like Asmita have been confined to a pre-determined gender mold. Like a frog that fell into it, unable to climb back, seeing only what others desire.

Scapegoating Western Nepal with Prejudice

Chhaupadi refers to Chhau (blood) and padi (condition). Looking at the accusatory remarks, all fingers seem to point towards Western Nepal, declaring it an exclusive Chhaupadi zone. No doubt Western Nepal has been tagged with prejudice and menstrual discrimination. In fact, even though how and to what extent they observe might differ, Chhaupadi is everywhere in the world where there are Nepalis. The essence after all is same-discrimination against women. The word Chhaupadi targets Western Nepal indiscriminately; instead, a broader term "menstrual discrimination" which circumscribes the universal picture is contextual.

On top of that, the practice of isolating postpartum women in sheds and depriving human contact is also invoked as Chhaupadi, not to mention its association with mother and child's health. Thus, the issue of the malpractice is obfuscated by irrelevant terms to deliberately garner more weight at the cost of issues which should have been highlighted. Chhaupadi is more blood-related and pertains to menstruation and/or postpartum situation.

There are more women who menstruate than who deliver babies. While a woman in her lifetime menstruates for up to six years in average (more than 2340 days), she observes postpartum days only for sixty-six days even if she delivers six babies in her lifetime and observes each for eleven consecutive days, after which the child undergoes Nwaran (the naming ceremony). Postpartum and menstrual states are different conditions and should not be coalesced to one description.

Postpartum issues began to garner attention all over since 1998, when Safe Motherhood program was being piloted in Nepal. Unfortunately, there was no say on menstruation. Even though the program admitted that adolescence was a part of reproductive health, no one felt the need to discuss it further. Ashamed?

Today, safe motherhood program has achieved a lot. No matter how grave both issues are, they deserve equal attention in separate categories. However, menstruation and postpartum practices are both deemed as Chhaupadi practices while they are inherently different concepts. Dignified menstruation contributes to safe motherhood to a larger extent; the latter only adds to it. Hence, keeping them in one basket, at least in Nepali perspective, is a typological failure.

Furthermore, those activists who are working on such fields do not choose what is pertinent but only what comforts them. What we observe as a bystander can be different from what the reality is on the ground. Declaring Chhaupadi sheds as dirty without understanding ground reality is paving another way of building 'clean' Chaau sheds-which became a reality with the collaboration of certain governmental and non-governmental agencies, to the apprehension of many. There is no difference between Chhaupadi sheds of villages and that of five-star hotel rooms, which have been the latest trend amongst the well-to-do orthodoxies. As documented on Dec 11, 2018, in a seminar organized by MHM alliance (a network of organizations that work on menstruation health and sanitation)-a five-star hotel's second floor witnessed state-of-the-art Chhaupadi shed for the affluent. When the news came to the media, it raised serious questions as to what was problematic: the rustic nature of Chhaupadi sheds or the unlawful seclusion? Which shed was dirtier?

A majority of people who depend on hand-to-mouth sustenance have to work daily and live in the rustic surroundings they are the part of. They neither have extravagant dining tables to feed nor fancy clothes to wear. Sometimes, they have to live by without water and most of the time without knowledge. Dirt is a relative word when it comes to hygiene. For some, mud and cow dung may be counted as dirt, but for many, they mean business. When activists complain those women feed in dire circumstances during menstruation, they must understand that they feed like that under all circumstances. The problem is not really feeding sanitation but living conditions because of poverty. They place their chapatis over their mud hearth and devour on them, and sometimes over their 'dirty' clothes they've worn for days.

Unfortunately for these people, what is 'dirtier' than their living conditions is their woman's blood because of which they restrict their contact with home, food, and many other things. Instead of addressing the dread of secluding women to sheds and treating them as second-class human beings, the sanitary aspect is more centered. Not that it's not important-but the issue is generalized while specifics are highlighted. Patronizing and trivializing their living styles and economic limitations is, for me, perpetrating prejudice against the people of entire Western Nepal.

Crying for the demolition of Chhaupadi sheds and calling for constructing common, clean sheds without ameliorating their living conditions and preserving dignity is gross insensitivity. Furthermore, arguing that building Chhaupadi residence in five-star hotel rooms will allow the privileged to empathize with the poor is equally futile, even outrageous. This does nothing than institutionalize Chhaupadi through all means in all social strata.

To ensure the right to dignified menstruation, and living in general, the lowest common denominator should be that girls and women must not be separated from their families for whatever reason. Instead of growing prejudices against a community, class, or geographical region, it is more logical to educate people on scientific understanding of menstruation and the rights Nepal's constitution has guaranteed. If we can do so, the community will have only two modes of living: to live like a human or an animal. Destroying chhaupadi sheds in the hearts and minds of the people should precede destroying chhaupadi sheds at homes. When we're able to do that, we will have destroyed this ill tradition for good. There is no point in campaigning to destroy sheds which have been built with hard-earned money because they can always be used to store grains and fodder for animals. The sheds would essentially be demolished the day we'll destroy chhaupadi from the minds of the people.

We have been cold towards the plight of our sisters and mothers: we either watched them in utter indifference or brushed it aside altogether. We didn't have enough courage to speak for our daughters, sisters, and mothers, and that's a fact. Those who did-we deemed them agents of social sabotage. When the foreigners started to speak against it, the dollars came in. And then we started misappropriating it for something we felt comfortable. If this is not what we should be ashamed of, what is?

If we want to understand Nepal, we have to go to the villages. If we want to understand our daughters' and mothers' menstrual plights, we really have to go there. If we want to bring a change in society, we really have to go to the villages. We have to sleep in those sheds, listen to the songs of dignity that shred inside, and before all that, live that life ourselves.

A malpractice further fuels with mutual conformity. Our grandparents didn't allow our parents to be a seed of change and they did the same to us. Now we're supposed to do the same to each other. Our relations should be as good as our love for each other, not as bad as our ill traditions. Change needs a force and we're reluctant to use it, which is nowhere but inside us. Just a push is needed and we can break it easily in baby steps. But we don't have time for it. It takes much time and energy to visit Western Nepal and we're afraid to let our inner monsters loose. We're afraid that our shoes might bring that dirt to our immaculate homes. We're afraid that the practice is contagious; the people are contagious. We're afraid that our hearts will reek of the stinky truth that sits in the corner of our houses. And thus, we built our sheds in multi-star hotels and elaborate rooms. Well, it took nothing to do it: just spend some money, click a selfie of the rooms, and post it for everyone to see.

We are ashamed to go to Mahottari, Chitwan, or Kapilvastu to observe the ground reality because that's exactly what we have been doing, only with more money and less extravagance, and differently, in a way that suits us. And we never fail to sing the hymns of change that will be brought one day but will be slow, steady, and perpetual if we wait enough for it. I think the argument that change is slow is lame. Change is only as far as our intentions and as late as our actions. But we do not invest on the resources that bring the kind of change we think will come-investment in education and investment in science and technology. Scientific thinking will indeed make us more enlightening but it doesn't entail the outright rejection of traditions. In fact, only those traditions and cultures that enhance our living and dignity are truly ours. The rest are the baggage we've picked up on the way, like a child who picked dirt and is now reluctant to give it up. Change is only as far as this. It is indeed incapacitating-in fact, crippling-to wait for change no one takes the initiative of. Who else will speak if not us when our grandparents still believe in it? We can't change them in entirety and our parents are stuck between our grannies and their own children. In that case, should we be the ones who're to carry the baton to this tradition? The new generation is mostly affected from this. We must speak and for change. We have to choose whether we want to give our daughters a book on one hand or stuffed cloth on the other. We can't let our daughters be the victims of the same plight. We can't let the past ruin our future. We just can't.

The reason Nepal has not made significant strides in development as compared to other countries is as plain as daylight. Some rich and the powerful chose to be the marionettes of the donors while the others made the donors that. The donors know exactly what they wanted and they've been playing the puppeteer at the cost of few bucks and namastes and God knows what. In an attempt of painting the political parties and its leaders in slimes of reproach, activists and organizations alike have publicly displayed their white tusks of transformational façade while disrupting societies by pandering on their whim. The ignorance of international media which tagged Western Nepal to chhaupadi unjustly did so without caring to investigate the reality. Worse, the

Nepali social intelligentsia ignored it like a wind that passes by. Well, we have made the word chhaupadi global but along with it painted Western Nepal with notoriety.

***

Bangkok Airport.

Stakeholders from all over the globe gathered in the airport to participate in a training which was to make males responsible, in order to mitigate gender-based violence. Amid the introduction going on among the delegates, a Sudanese male delegate turned toward me and said, “May I ask a question if you don’t mind?”

“Sure, please go on,” I said. “I bet you’re talking about our constitutional process. As soon as we’ll wrap up this event, the leaders will come to an understanding. This has always been the case.”

“No, that was not it,” he said smiling. “I don’t understand your country’s politics.”

What more do you need to be embarrassed? I berated myself for being incessantly predictive.

“I’ve read that people evict menstruating daughters from their houses in your country. Is it true? And does it still happen?” he asked.

I nodded in agreement, couldn’t be embarrassed more.

The discussion continued throughout the training.

When I say that the issue of menstruation was not first raised by any Nepali human rights activists, I claim so with full responsibility. Only after the issue raised extraneously, Nepali activists took it over. Not that there aren't women who could do that, there are-many participating in United Nations programs delegating from Nepal, in programs of Ministries, Councils, and that of UN Women. But they had merely raised this issue because they never wanted to offend or challenge anyone. It is indeed amusing to hear them say that menstruation is not a matter of peace and empowerment. They do not intend to admit that the society has not allowed menstruating women in participating in any programs-be it local peace committees or the meetings of rural municipalities. For them, a successful project is realized only if you can articulate your agenda by (mis) appropriating twisted realities in perfect English and make the donor continue to pay in delight. Instead of taking the issues that are suited to the country, they globalized it, saw things here and now with the heart thousands of kilometers away.

In March, 2017, when Shanta Adhikari spoke representing Radha Paudel Foundation in the United States, in the 61st session of Commission on the Status of Women (CSW61), the Nepalis present there bellowed her. They accused her of shaming the country.

"There are women all over in top positions in Nepal. Don't you perpetuate lies," they said.

Well, if the news of daughters dying of snake bites in animal sheds because of reaching reproductive age doesn't shame the country, and voicing against it does, then there's nothing to say.

Nepali people have fought gender wars and advocated women's participation in top positions to prioritize women's power, capability, needs, and aspirations, not to keep their mouth shut when daughters are dying for nothing. We have also not sent women representatives in the parliament just because they shout yay to their male counterparts' or their parties' whim. And definitely not to berate another woman on speaking for women.

***

I sent an application for conducting a 3-hour-workshop for Asia Pacific Forum on Women, Law, and Development (APWLD) in 2017. It was accepted. But I had to collaborate with an organization called Sankalpa because our agendas were similar. The issue I had raised was how menstrual traditions impact the achievements of Peace and Sustainable Development Goals 2030 and where we, the activists, went wrong.

After we met Sankalpa's employee and reached an understanding, I was headed for Dailekh district. What astonished me was in a week time Sankalpa changed course and formulated new plans without our consent. They wrote to the organizer that I was indifferent to the collaboration. While we had planned to merge ideas, they had been planning for a split, and that too without offering me an opportunity to participate.

I was numbed for long and could not come with a response. But I chose not to keep quiet. I shot an email to the organizer expounding them about the latest developments. Without hesitation, I wrote, "this is the evidence how women with all the money, an English tongue, and political power can squash and bully other activists." I carbon-copied the email and sent it to all the stakeholders. It created a hullaballoo all around-from Bangkok to Nepal. I still chose not to back out from my stance. In two hours, I grabbed my visa and booked a flight to Chiang Mai, Thailand, for the presentation.

When I reached there, I urged them repetitively for a collaborative meeting before the presentation. At last, they agreed to meet one day before. I sat there waiting for them but they never came. It was time to give a presentation without preparation. One of the Ps of the 3Ps had been left out.

We had a thematic mismatch in our agendas-that of my foundation and Sankalpa's. I had to present jostling against the agendas of people whom I had considered were my own from the very beginning.

Whether it is Kathmandu or Philippines, Bangkok or New York, Nepali elite communities barely want to speak out. Or they cannot, on menstruation. Like it is not worth their attention.

In 2018, some activists started to speak out but they resorted to the term "traditional harmful practices" instead of what it actually is: menstruation. Menstruation yet again was buried in the heap of generalized classificatory tropes. Yet again, the elephant in the room was obscured in shrouds of euphemism.

Menstrual Hygiene Day

Since 2014, the 28th of the fifth month of every year, that is May, is observed as Menstrual Hygiene Day in various shapes and forms in Nepal. The fifth month May is taken to signify in average five days of menstruation. It is observed on 28th of May because it represents the 28-day cycle on average in the interludes of which most women menstruate.

After United Nations declared that menstrual practices are a major hurdle in achieving gender equality-that was in 2014-menstruation garnered attention in the history of global development, albeit on a miniscule magnitude. A biological phenomenon female experience due to which life has sustained on earth took centuries to grab attention-how about that? Sadly, dignified menstruation seems to be in its early childhood.

A brief look into the history of human rights won't take us farther than 1948. Since the declaration of Convention on the Elimination of All Forms of Discrimination Against Women, 1979, substantial work has been done, similarly, on women's rights and empowerment. But unfortunately, it seems, menstruation did not deserve enough attention there, too. Especially after WWII, regions like the US, Europe, and Australia made huge strides in political, social, technical, and medical development. Menstruation, in these countries, is well accepted even though we don't see the debates in the public domain.

I was in the United States in 2012 and the elections were approaching. I sat by the television to learn more on the presidential candidates when an advertisement interrupted the show. A menstrual pad elegantly hurled around on which deep blue solution spilled. At first glance, it seemed to be perfectly fine to cater to all kinds of audience. But what bothered me was: are we really ashamed of the deep red color of menstrual blood? How can television which shows explicit content of violence step back when it comes to harmless blood that gives birth to human beings?

The word menstruation seems to have been in limelight since the advocacy of reproductive rights. But to this day, its practice and impacts on living have never been discussed seriously with intent. Globally, menstruation still remains not just a taken-for-granted phenomenon, but also a mute non-disclosure agreement. Women too failed to articulate on this because of obvious social, economic, and political power dynamics. While men see this as a taboo, limited to "personal problems" of females, the world tagged menstruation in emotions that evoke shame and guilt. It was considered something that shouldn't be disclosed or declared.

In the yesteryears, women rarely participated in the United Nations and even if they did, only elite women from economically and social privileged class made it. These women too failed to project menstrual practices as a problem, something that should have been associated with dignity and rights. I have personally conversed with representatives from the various developmental partner organizations, who worked in Mugu and Bajura in 1985, but they then slept in sheds when they menstruated. This is not what true women representation, or worse, national representation looks like. Preaching without practice cannot be praiseworthy.

They could not associate menstruation with women's rights, or didn't realize, to say the least. They were patriarchal-ized into such socialization and in some cases even the approaches of anthropologists and socialists was orthodox.

Taking into account the history of this day, whenever people from developed countries visited Africa and Asia and saw the horrendous conditions girls and women were in-packed in claustrophobic sheds separate from their families, skipping school days to survive water-less, unhygienic toilets-they conducted small pads and toilet charities, and that's how it all started. They wrote an account of it and advocated for the rights of these women. This eventually kicked into a sanitary campaign and was limited to it since.

With such a hype from foreigners, the 'insiders' launched the campaigns and advocacies triggered, 'spontaneously' from within. The campaigns run by foreigners garnered adequate attention. From 2014, a German-led NGO called WASH United started celebrating 28th of May as Menstruation Hygiene Day. Its partner organization, organizations influenced by it, and people inspired by it also followed the practice. To this day, there are more than forty people and organizations associated with the NGO which have been celebrating it continually. This campaign alone cannot address the impacts in the sectoral, social, economic, psychological, physiological, political, environmental, personal, familial, and national level whether in developed, developing or underdeveloped countries.

In the context of Nepal, there are more than forty actions or items on which there are undeclared prohibitions.

These items range from clothes women wear during menstruation, food they ought to eat to people they must stay away from. There is no doubt that hygiene is crucial to menstruation but this cannot be the complete picture. That-girls and women get clean toilets and menstrual pads doesn't mean they will live a dignified life.

Hygienic menstruation doesn't necessarily equate with dignified menstruation.

So, such programs cannot guarantee the right to freedom of movement, right to equality, right against discrimination, right to food, right to health, and many other rights safeguarded in the books of constitution and international laws.

By the same token, a clean house, be it in Western Nepal, Kathmandu, or Britain, cannot guarantee these rights. Menstruating women and girls in both clean and dirty houses are barred from doing certain activities. It is always the fear game the society plays-that something might happen to someone if they do this and that.

Likewise, the growing trend of distributing free menstrual pads in Nepal also bases its intent on achieving hygienic menstruation; it doesn't completely address the questions of dignified menstruation though. Contrary to it, this act stifles the right of women to choose a menstrual product. Dependency on costly goods and the environmental pollution it causes are the other aspects it doesn't address.

Menstruation malpractices impacts both short- and long-term goals on women, family, society, peace, rights, empowerment, education, health, water supply, and environment, which is a prerequisite to achieving dignified menstruation. Unless and until any such efforts are prioritized to intervene in all the multi-dimensional aspects of menstruation, the mandatory aspects of dignified menstruation are far from materialization. If left unaddressed, menstrual practices will impede a country's attainment of peace and progress. All in all, the mere idea of hygienic menstruation as a full picture is incomplete, lopsided, prejudiced, and unilateral.

When it comes to practice in Nepal, most of the menstruation-based activism appear to be biased. It was merely a valid issue for either the politicians or the activists irrespective of gender. After the restoration of democracy, though substantial works on women empowerment, human rights, peace and sanitation had been done, most of them were imported and yoked issues. Issues pertinent to Nepal were barely looked at.

Since the age of five or so, both boys and girls experience (girls endure) the prohibitive practices observed by women in their houses and neighborhood and wake up to the gender divide of powerful and powerless categories. Boys and girls then categorize themselves into these society-dictated groups and are socialized into these stereotypes. This has not just furthered the chasm between males and females, but also promoted and perpetuated violence of all kinds against women, especially social, physical, psychological, sexual, and economic. Regrettably, instead of delving deeper into the root causes of the violence, most of the actions have taken course to superficial wandering, contrary to what has been mandated by political transformations and women movement.

When our daughters die in sheds but Nepali rights activists choose to keep mute to the issue, the country with the tallest mountain Sagarmatha nods in shame. Those who've spoken owing to international pressure have been zombified to the old tradition of restricting outreach to the menstrual debate, which in itself is sad. The policies and programs brought upon by the then full-majority 2018 Communist government also limited the serious issue of menstruation in the sense of 'like ill-tradition', which proves either they aren't aware of the truth or simply choose not to be bothered by it.

The then Ministry of Water Supply and Sanitation had led the issue of menstrual sanitation and done some praiseworthy works, if seen in isolation. However, that doesn't suffice. The toilets which have been constructed under the Open-Defecation-Free campaign could not ensure women's dignity. Toilets were narrow and thus gender-limited. They were not appropriate for usage for girls and women especially for changing their clothes. There was no arrangement for proper disposal of menstrual products, no soaps, not even water in many of them. In some toilets, there were no doors. If doors, no latches. In many places, women and girls were prohibited for the usage of these toilets. Needless to say, this campaign was run heeding to Sustainable Development Goal 6.2: to achieve access to adequate and equitable sanitation for all. But it is far in reach from assimilating the pragmatic dimensions of dignified menstruation. This campaign seems to be overpowered more by organizations which had already been working on drinking water supply and sanitation.

Dignity doesn't necessarily come from superficial purity. Without demolishing the chhaupadi sheds of

Kathmandu, the crusade for self-respect cannot be accomplished and thus the integrated and long-term solution will still lurk around in the dark. It is a form of gender apartheid-menstrual seclusion. Be it chhaupadi sheds, animal sheds, or concrete or bamboo walls, it is still away from home and honor. Whether under concrete buildings or treacherous billets, tucked in warm beds or shivering in cold plastic, concealing women in a separate place due to menstruation can never be considered a dignified stay.

When it comes to taking menstruation as an issue, except for one organization among the surveyed fourteen which observed Menstruation Day in 2017, none raised the issue of dignified menstrual Hygiene on their report review. Most of them concentrated on sanitation and sanitary materials. Furthermore, the 2018 committee formed to observe Menstruation Day also seems to back the same trend. Despite being the integrated program of Women, Education, and Health Ministry, the participation of organizations that worked in peace, empowerment, human rights, health, and education was almost non-existent.

If the government continues to play indifferent to the plight of women and along with it, organizations continue to treat menstrual discrimination as a mere harmful tradition, no significant progress can ever be made. Unlike menstruation practices of Africa, which is poverty-ridden, and Bangladesh and Pakistan, which are aggravated by poverty and taboo alike, Nepal's nature of the problem is undoubtedly rooted in poverty but perpetrated more by religion, culture, and gender discrimination.

Despite all these challenges, there is still unprecedented opportunity for us to bring progress in the discussion, debate, and performance toward dignified menstruation. Nepal government has already planted the seed towards its achievement, even though embryonic and fragmentary. In this regard, Ministry of Water Supply finally drafted the policy document for dignified menstruation as of 2017. We should address this problem both intensively and aggressively. It is not enough that the international community is still intrigued and willing and Nepal government's hunger for fast-paced development is still on; without the realization of dignity in women's life, there is no way their wholesome issues will be addressed. On the whole, dignified menstruation should not remain an option or an opportunistic invention. It is and should be everyone's issue, not just pertaining to a certain geographical region, community, or gender. We have to learn to step up beyond our religious, cultural, gender, and socioeconomic vested interests in order to subdue their overwhelming and complicated nature.

In a nutshell, the day when our local political leaders will be willing to ensure women and girls of every nook a dignified living during menstruation, our dream of a prosperous, peaceful, and a just Nepal will be materialized in its true sense. Dignified menstruation, again, is not an option but a mandatory clause for achieving our targets of Sustainable Development Goals, hunger, poverty, education, health, and gender equality issues. Menstruation-related (mal)practices are not an exclusive issue of women but a social and moral transgression that has to be tamed. It is a human problem by every means: every bit of menstruation-related rights are human rights. It is high time we now discussed and debated it in both public and private spaces. The initiation should be taken by family members, both males and females, in private spaces. Our mothers, daughters, sisters, and wives deserve much more than this. We swept their plights under rugs for a long time. They deserve love, value, and dignity, not lust, sheds, and shame. Dignified Menstruation is as important an issue as human rights and is must everybody's responsibility, not just women's. Therefore, the discussion or talk or dialogue on dignified menstruation should initiate from every family. Dignified Menstruation should be personalized and politicatized.

Translator's Note

I won't put forward another argument the writer only has the expertise of because it would be a trivial attempt on my part. Rather, I'd like to point out a never-talked-of aspect of this book which is equally commendable.

When I first read this book, I felt distant, unable to relate to the writer's agony. But the more I flipped through the pages, the more empathetic I grew, and somewhere towards the middle of the book, I bled. And from deep down. Not from the uterine deep that I do not possess but from realizing things-said to be so understood, yet misunderstood-are taken for granted both by the so-called intellectually affluent and impoverished.

As I turned the last page, I had the epiphany that this was the book I was looking for all along that I could cherish. Not because it had all the perfect elements of creative non-fiction but because it is one of the first-the first attempt at formal science communication from a Nepali stage. This is as much a document of scientific communication as it is of advocacy of women's rights, human rights, dignified menstruation, and environmentalism.

From dawn to dusk in history, we've had all the poetic and artistic inspiration from aesthetically pleasing writers who plucked the moon from the sky and petted at home but none of the writers who dared to communicate the science behind superstition, in a matter-of-fact tone. Education, awareness, and scientific realization in a country like ours are true needs the attainment of which will only substantiate our taste in literature. That said, I neither intend to criticize art-for-art's sake nor hierarchize forms of literature into tropes of mine and definitely not intend to advocate utilitarian literature. But it is worth acknowledging that when the western publishing frontier has been communicating bleeding-edge science to the world-quantum mechanics, evolution, and cosmic discoveries-we're at least starting from the wounds that pain us.

I wish more books, both fiction and non-fiction, came to educate people in the true sense and not just amuse them in delight. The attempt of the writer to communicate Dignified Menstruation both in ethical terms and through science deserves both acclamation and claps.

Editor/Translator
Umesh Bajagain

Reviewers

Although women all over the world menstruate during a large part of their lives, the topic is nevertheless surrounded with stigma and shame. Sometimes this is in the name of religion, sometimes it is due to social norms. Radha Paudel has written a very important book on the impact of traditions that shame and limit the way that women live during their periods. She vividly and colorfully describes life in Nepal where in some places women and girls are sometimes forced to live in cow sheds during menstruation, with their health - and sometimes even their lives - at risk. How can traditions and social norms be changed so that women and girls can live truly dignified lives? These are fundamental questions that Radha is exploring in her book. I recommend this book to anyone who is interested in reproductive health rights, women's rights or life in Nepal more generally.

Annette Lyth,

Chief of Office, Office of the Special Representative of the Secretary General on Violence against Children

The trials and tribulations of womanhood - the celebrations, the challenges, the joys and pains are universal. Radha Paudel's Apabitra Ragat brings these to life in her Nepali tapestry of colour and texture . She explores the rites of passage from girlhood to womanhood in the company of sisters alike– "Each woman finds the other her own. Each sees in the other her self. Glad and gleaming at least for this day. " Beautifully written, and a joy to read. A unique advocacy for the celebration of menstruation and a challenge to the dominant discourse of women's lives.

Emma Leslie, Executive Director, Centre for Peace and Conflict Studies

Apabitra Ragat (Im/Pure Blood) tells Radha Paudel's passionate journey and relentless fight for dignified menstruation in Nepal and worldwide. Having herself a traumatising experience with menstruation, Paudel decided to work as a trained nurse in the remote villages of Jumla, in the Western region of Nepal, where she witnessed menstrual malpractices such as Chhaupadi, in which women are banished to cow shed once a month. The restrictions imposed on women and girls during their menstruation and the impact these have on their physical and mental wellbeing symbolise entrenched gender inequality not just in Jumla, but all over Nepal.

As dignified menstruation is a matter of equality, we all need to speak up for women's dignity and raise awareness to break down the menstruation 'sheds' in people's minds. Menstruation is not only a women's issue, but also a political and human rights issue!

Françoise Binsfeld, Gender and Sustainable Development specialist, Luxembourg, Europe

www.ingramcontent.com/pod-product-compliance
Lightning Source LLC
LaVergne TN
LVHW091304150826
845673LV00006B/1532

9789937131940